ECHO
STORIES
for Children

Celebrating Saints and Seasons in Word and Action

PAGE McKEAN ZYROMSKI

XXIII

TWENTY-THIRD PUBLICATIONS
Mystic, CT 06355

Twenty-Third Publications
185 Willow Street
P.O. Box 180
Mystic, CT 06355
(860) 536-2611
(800) 321-0411

ISBN 0-89622-930-0
Library of Congress Catalog Card Number 98-60312
Printed in the U.S.A.

Table of Contents

Echo Stories for Children

Introduction

Echo stories are my favorite way of teaching, hands down *(sweep arms widely)*. The kids are on their feet, stomping and gesturing and contorting their faces *(wrinkle nose, roll eyes heavenward)*. They repeat each line after me in an itty-bitty voice, or a full-throated growl, or a whisper, or a shout *(place hands around mouth like megaphone)*. They do their best to imitate my gestures and actions exactly. When they can't quite manage it *(snap your fingers, whistle)*, nobody minds because we're all too busy, we're all in it together, we want to get on with the *story*.

The echo stories in this book are arranged to move through the school year, September to June, highlighting liturgical seasons, feast days of various saints, and holidays. I wanted them to be dependable of course, in terms of theology and history, but I also wanted a lively tale or two from the church's vast storehouse of legend and popular devotion. So you'll meet St. Francis' Wolf of Gubbio, who very likely *is* historical (but wonderfully embellished), and in the same month you'll meet Jack-o'-Lantern, who definitely *is not* historical, but who has more name recognition among children than the President of the United States (even though the morality tale behind his Halloween grin is all but forgotten).

How do you *use* echo stories? You probably suspect that you'll need to be a cheerleader of sorts, maybe even an aerobics instructor: "Now everybody, stand up, stretch your legs! You're going to repeat every line I say in the same tone of voice, and you're going to imitate every action I make just as I do it! Now, let's GO!"

That's a big part of it. Your enthusiasm (or lack of it) will be caught and mirrored back to you. Using an echo story is not a spur of the moment choice. I usually tell teachers to photocopy the script for themselves so they can fold it in half to hold in one hand. A book is too bulky to hold while contorting, and the only people who've told me they *memorize* the scripts have been clown ministers in front of large intergenerational audiences. (But if you're fond of memorizing, more power to you.)

In any case the scripts need to be tailored to *your* immediate situation. As you rehearse, mark up your photocopy, highlight it, color code it—anything to make the phrasings *personal*. When you introduce yourself as "Saint N." in the "All Saints" echo story, make sure you write your own name so you don't stumble at the last minute (your mind will be on a dozen things, I guarantee). If your parish doesn't have a "Rice Bowl" tradition for Lent, delete that whole business in "Ashes, Ashes" and substitute the name of *your* parish's program. Each time I use one of these scripts for a new audience, I go through the whole process of tailoring all over again, which is another reason I never mark in the book itself.

I've tried to fill each echo story with specific details that will bring them alive for the "ordinary" parish and the "ordinary" classroom, but the price of specific details is that they need to be changed to fit *your* "ordinary" situation (which is never "ordinary," right?). A Protestant friend of mine asked if she could use "Moses and the People Who Grumbled" and change the eucharistic references. That particular piece seems to me to be about as eucharistic as it gets, but ecumenical relations are such that I was delighted she found something useful and that her class loved it.

The Mood of Your Class

Another part of tailoring these echo stories is the need to scale them to the mood of your class and the next thing on their agenda. If it's the tenth day of rain in a row, the class will want to whoop and holler a bit, but they *must* settle down enough to finish the school day without driving you bananas.

To this purpose, you need to know there are basically two ways of ending all echo stories: by repeating the last few lines faster and LOUDER, building to a SHOUT; or by repeating the last few lines more and more softly and s-l-o-w-l-y, ending by whispering or mouthing the words silently. Obviously the first method is fine when you're sending your class into the arena to face the lions (or out to recess). The second is what you're more likely to choose when your nerves are frazzled.

Another thing to note while you're tailoring is whether the actions are too vigorous for you at the moment. If you're wearing high heels and a straight skirt, you may not want to "fall to the ground" when St. Paul gets knocked off his high horse (much less "stick your feet in the air" when Paul's prison shackles miraculously fall off—this teaching method is not for the fainthearted!). You'll want to make your actions as broad and dramatic as possible, but you must know ahead of time that you'll "fall to your knees," or "tug at your socks" with St. Nicholas, or "fold up the front of your sweater/tilma" with Juan Diego at Guadalupe. Studying up, practicing, then adapting the phrasings and the actions to *your* needs will keep you from unwelcome surprises midstream.

What age groups are these for? Now, this is an interesting question, and I never know quite how to answer. I originally intended them for K–4, but my friends who are clown ministers have opened a new audience for me. This type of storytelling is a success with a diverse mix, especially intergenerational groups. Adults are enthusiastic about standing up and going through these stories when children or grandchildren are at their sides. Retreat groups like them. Even the tough junior high audience will "play along" when they're partnered with young children, the way some parishes link first communion children with confirmandi, for example. And who do you think learns the most from these "childish activities"? You guessed it.

A Variety of Uses

Most parishes have more *intergenerational* catechetical moments than they realize, and I urge you to use echo stories for ice breakers or for the Shrove Tuesday pancake supper or for the Grandparents' Day luncheon. Individual echo stories are also useful on occasions other than their calendar celebrations. "St. Joseph Was a Carpenter," for instance, would be appropriate around Labor Day or on May 1, in addition to March 19, his feast day. "Moses and the People Who Grumbled" serves nicely for first communion preparation. "Mary's Story" can be used almost any time.

About half of these echo stories appeared first in *Catechist* magazine, and I thank editor and friend Pat Fischer for all her suggestions in our ten years of developing the format. I also thank the teachers who used the scripts and called or wrote to me with further tips.

Because of all this practical advice from many quarters, you'll find that each echo story in this collection is preceded by general interest notes to help you with an informal introduction, and followed by a few discussion questions and an informal closing prayer. None of these are written in stone, they're just to give you ideas and spur your own spontaneity. I repeat my firm conviction that *you* are the only one who knows how to make the adaptations for *your* class. You alone know whether you need to explain vocabulary words like "martyr," "missionary," "bishop," or whether "Ireland" and "Mexico" have special meaning for your students.

I hope you'll find these suggestions helpful, but please add your own way of concretizing the stories by bringing maps, or pictures of Our Lady of Guadalupe or Abraham Lincoln, or even matzoh crackers for "Passover and the Last Supper." In short, put your own stamp on these little scripts, give them your very own ZIP code, and meanwhile, everybody stand UP! Let's GO! *(jog briskly in place).*

Angels, Angels, Everywhere

"Angel" is from the Greek word meaning "messenger," which is only one way these supernatural beings serve our loving God. ("Angel" is what they do, says St. Augustine; "spirit" is what they are.) Popular interest in angels is high right now but the Church has always honored their significant role, as we see in the Bible and in their feasts on the liturgical calendar. Early Christian artists portrayed angels simply as young men. The addition of wings was a later development. September 29 is the feast of the three archangels named in Scripture—Michael, Gabriel, and Raphael—and October 2 is the feast of the Guardian Angels: two opportunities to remind students that "God has put his angels in charge of you, to guard you in all your ways" (Psalm 91:11).

God's angels are everywhere.
(flap arms as if wings)

Just because we can't see them,
(cover eyes, try to peek)

doesn't mean they aren't there.
(point to corners of room)

The *Bible* talks about angels,
(open palms together, as if reading book)

From the first book...to the last.
(place right palm on left for "first," flip over for "last")

An angel wrestles all night with Jacob...
(wrap arms around self, pretend to "wrestle")

An angel is with Daniel in the lion's den...
(growl, make claws of hands)

An angel helps Peter and John escape from prison...
(turn to the side, then tiptoe stealthily)

Angels surround the *whole life* of Jesus—
(turn 360 degrees, sweeping arms)

from before he was born...
(rock "baby" in arms)

till he ascended into heaven.
(lift hands together up to the heavens)

Gabriel is one of the angels.
(flap arms like wings)

You can read about him in Luke's gospel.
(open palms together as if reading book)

He announces the birth of Jesus to Mary.
(rock "baby" in arms)

And the birth of John the Baptist before that.
(rock arms even faster)

And if you read the book of Daniel,
(open palms together as if reading book)

you'll see that Gabriel helps Daniel two times
(hold up two fingers)

in understanding his strange visions.
(put both fists under chin, frown, pondering)

Three times an angel comes to St. Joseph in dreams...
(hold up three fingers)

Once to tell about the birth of Jesus...
(rock arms, holding baby)

Once to warn him to flee to Egypt...
(turn to the side, run in place)

And once to tell him it was safe to come home.
(turn in opposite direction, trot briskly)

Another famous angel is Michael.
(flap arms like wings)

He's the "mighty prince" of angels.
(flex muscles in arms)

He watches over the Church and guards it.
(shade eyes with hand, gaze out in all directions)

He's the leader of the heavenly hosts in battle.
(pretend to have a sword fight)

You can read about Michael in the book of Daniel,
(open palms together as if reading book)

and in the book of Revelation.
(move hands to another position, open and read book)

God's angels are everywhere!
(sweeping motions with hands, everywhere)

Raphael is another angel.
(flap arms as if wings)

You can read about him in the book of Tobit.
(open hands as if reading book)

He travels along with Tobit's son on a trip,
(saunter in place, whistle)

and protects him from harm,
(hold arms out like safety patrol for schoolchildren)

and heals Tobit's blindness.
(cover eyes with hand, suddenly remove and blink)

Those three angels are the only ones
(hold up three fingers, tick them off)

whose *names* we know from the Bible.
(open hands as if reading book)

But Jesus talks about our *guardian angels*,
(flap arms as if wings)

who are always in the presence of God.
(point to heaven)

They protect us
(hold out arms like safety patrol for schoolchildren)

and lead us to life.
(reach out hand and "tug," leading)

Angels are messengers and servants of God.
(point up to heaven)

Their song, "Glory to God in the highest..."
(raise arms in praise)

has never stopped echoing on earth.
(shake head)

God's angels are everywhere!
(sweeping motions with hands, "everywhere")

Just because we can't see them,
(cover eyes, try to peek)

doesn't mean they aren't there...
(point to corners of room)

or there...or there...
(point closer to people)

or here...
(point by your own side)

Let's thank God for the help of angels!
(flap arms like wings)

Let's join them in giving God praise!
(raise arms high in praise of God)

Questions for Discussion

After the students sit down, use these questions to start a discussion:

- Have you seen any television programs or movies about angels? How do they act as God's messengers?

- Why do angels need to say, "Don't be afraid," or "Fear not," when they first appear to someone?

- Why do you think artists draw angels with wings?

- Do heavenly beings really need wings?

- Do you ever ask for help from your guardian angel, or pray that God sends angels to protect you? Try to learn this prayer by heart:

  Angel of God, my guardian dear,
  To whom God's love commits me here.
  Ever this day be at my side,
  to light, to guard, to rule, and guide. Amen.

Closing Prayer

Lord Jesus, we pray that you send your angels to guard us in all our ways and lead us closer to you. Give us a new appreciation for the angels, a new sense of wonder at the many ways you care for us. We ask that we may join them in singing their wonderful song forever, "Glory to God in the highest, glory to God in the highest!" Amen.

St. Thérèse, God's Little Flower

In 1997 Thérèse Martin was named a Doctor of the Church by Pope John Paul II. This title links her with thirty-three other saints—including Augustine, Thomas Aquinas, Albert the Great, and Teresa of Avila—honored for being "wise, holy, learned, and a source of sound teaching for the whole church." Yet Thérèse of Lisieux (1873–1897), the "Little Flower," died in complete obscurity at age twenty-four. Within twenty-five years of her death, however, her simple autobiography *The Story of a Soul* was selling millions of copies, translated into forty languages, even though it was written originally only for Carmelite nuns. With immediate and lasting impact, the "Little Way" that Thérèse outlined opened up the holiness of everyday life to ordinary people all over the globe. Thérèse is the patron saint of the Missions and of France. Her feast day is October 1. We use the English form of her name, Theresa, in this echo story because it's easier for most children to say.

Theresa Martin was God's *little* flower.
(with thumb and forefinger measure "little")

She always knew she was little.
(palm down, measure halfway to ground)

She was the baby of the family.
(rock arms as if holding a baby)

She had FOUR big sisters.
(hold up four fingers, count them off)

Her sisters played games with her.
(hopscotch: hop on one foot three times, then both feet, repeat)

And taught her how to pray.
(bow head, fold hands)

They took her fishing with their father.
(make "fishing" motions, casting out line and reeling it in)

And taught her to read the Bible.
(pretend to open book and read)

Everyone loved little Theresa.
(pucker up, make "smooch, smooch, smooch" sounds)

She even got a little bit spoiled.
(fold arms, stick out lower lip, pout)

But she always ran to say "I'm sorry."
(run in place, reach out hand for "wait, wait")

And she always asked forgiveness.
(hang head, praying hands, imploring)

Theresa wanted to be a *great saint* when she grew up.
(flex muscles in arm, stand proudly)

She wanted to sail the ocean as a missionary.
(draw "waves" in the air with hands)

Or maybe be a *martyr* for the love of Christ.
(slit throat with hand, droop head, close eyes)

She wanted to be EVERYTHING for God.
(sweep arms broadly: "everything")

But she was just little.
(measure halfway to ground with palm, sadly)

One day she was looking at her garden.
(shade eyes to look)

She saw big, beautiful flowers,
(indicate tall flowers)

and teeny, little ones.
(indicate teeny, tiny flowers with thumb and forefinger)

The *little* flowers were just as beautiful as the *big* ones.
(nod head vigorously)

She knew God loved *both* the same.
(nod head even more vigorously)

She told God she would be God's little flower.
(point to heaven, point to self, nod)

But then her mother died,
(close eyes, droop head)

and Theresa was sad.
(sad face)

And one big sister went into the convent,
(wave bye-bye, turn back and wave over shoulder, smiling)

and Theresa was even MORE sad.
(make sad face and pull corners of mouth down with fingers)

Then ANOTHER sister went into the convent,
(wave bye-bye, turn back and wave over shoulder, smiling)

and THAT made Theresa even sadder.
(pull down corners of mouth even more, droop shoulders)

She **wanted to go into the convent too!**
(tap chest, insisting "me too")

But everybody said, "No."
(shake head)

She was too little.
(measure halfway to ground with palm, sadly)

Why was she always too little?
(stamp foot, fold arms, pout)

Finally she was big enough to go into the convent.
(wave bye-bye, turn back, wave over shoulder, smiling)

Now there were THREE sisters in the convent.
(hold up three fingers, counting 1-2-3)

Theresa asked to sail the ocean as a missionary,
(draw "waves" in the air with hands)

but everybody said, "No."
(shake head)

Her health was not good enough.
(beat chest, cough)

So she *prayed hard* for missionaries instead.
(praying hands, eyes closed, face turned upward)

She thought of a LITTLE way to become a saint.
(indicate "little" with thumb and forefinger)

Every LITTLE thing she did each day,
(keep indicating "little" with thumb and forefinger)

she did out of love of God.
(hands over heart for "love")

Even when she picked up a *pin* from the floor,
(lean down to pick up a pin)

she did it for love of God,
(hands over heart for "love")

without getting *mad* at the person who dropped it.
(stick out tongue, waggle hands in ears)

When somebody splashed water in the laundry,
(flinch and duck as if being splashed)

she was patient out of love for God,
(hands over heart for love)

without getting *mad* at the person who splashed her.
(stick out tongue, waggle hands in ears)

Nothing was too little
(indicate "little" with thumb and forefinger)

to be offered with love to God.
(hands over heart on "love")

She said little "I-love-you" prayers to God,
(fold hands, mouth "I love you, I love you")

even when she didn't feel like it inside.
(scowl slightly)

***Nothing* was too little**
(indicate "little" with thumb and forefinger)

to be offered with love to God.
(hands over heart on "love")

This was Theresa's "Little Way"
(indicate "little" with thumb and forefinger)

of becoming a BIG saint.
(flex muscles, puff out chest)

Then she got very sick,
(pound chest, cough-cough)

and knew she soon would die.
(droop head, close eyes)

Her sisters made her write a book,
(writing motions)

about her "Little Way."
(indicate "little" with thumb and forefinger)

Theresa promised that after she died,
(droop head, close eyes)

she would spend her time in heaven
(point to sky)

doing good on earth,
(point to earth)

and pray so hard for people still here,
(folded hands, praying fervently)

that she would rain roses down from heaven.
(imitate falling rain, raising and lowering fluttering fingers)

Theresa DID become a big, big saint,
(flex muscles, puff out chest, use deep voice on "big")

because of her little, little way
(indicate "little" with thumb and forefinger, pitch voice high)

of bringing love into the world
(hands over heart on "love")

by picking up a pin from the floor,
(lean down to pick up pin)

all for the love of God.
(hands over heart)

St. Theresa taught everybody
(point all around to everybody)

you don't have to sail the ocean as a missionary,
(draw "waves" in the air with hands)

to become a great saint.
(flex muscles, puff out chest)

We can be saints right where we are
(point to ground, stomp)

by picking up a pin from the floor,
(lean down to pick up pin)

all for the love of God.
(hands over heart on "love")

EVERYTHING for the love of God.
(sweeping motions with hands for "everything")

Little, little things...
(indicate "little" with thumb and forefinger)

with a BIG, BIG love.
(make huge circle with your arms)

Little, little things...
(whisper, indicate "little" with thumb and forefinger)

with a BIG, BIG LOVE!
(very loud, make huge circle with arms)

Questions for Discussion

After the students are sitting down, make sure they know what "martyr" means before beginning your discussion.

- Name some big flowers that you've seen, then name little ones. Is either kind *prettier* than the other?

- Does your parish have a program to help the Missions? What can children do for it?

- Do you like to pray for other people, even people you don't know, like Theresa did? How can you make up "little" prayers for them?

- Can you think of ways to remind yourself to say little "I-love-you" prayers to God during the day even when you don't feel like it?

- What do you feel like when you pick up little things in secret for other people?

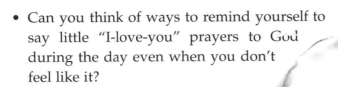

Closing Prayer

Lord Jesus, not everybody can be a missionary or a teacher or a martyr for you. But all of us *can* do little everyday things with a big, big love for you—even when we don't feel like it. Help us use St. Theresa's "Little Way" in our lives, and help us teach it to our friends and family. Thank you for showing us you love the shy little flowers in your garden just as much as the big fancy ones. Amen.

St. Francis and the Wolf of Gubbio

One of the most famous stories about the "Little Poor Man," St. Francis of Assisi (1182–1226), concerns a wolf who menaced the town of Gubbio in Italy. For years people thought this charming tale was merely a pious legend, but recently scholars have said it has more than a kernel of historical truth. A church, San Francesco della Pace, stands on the spot where Francis spoke to the wolf and where the wolf is buried. Francis regarded every creature on earth as his "brother" or "sister," because we are all made by the same heavenly Father. He especially loved the Incarnation of Jesus and his passion. Two popular customs which sprang from Francis' devotion are the crèche—or manger scene—at Christmastime, and the stations of the cross during Lent. Francis is the patron saint of ecology. His feast day is October 4.

Once upon a time, there was a big bad WOLF,
(growl, snarl, lift up "claws")

who prowled around a town named Gubbio.
("prowl," tiptoeing stealthily, growling)

He gobbled up stray chickens...
(cluck, cluck, cluck)

He gobbled up stray dogs...
(woof, woof, woof)

He gobbled up stray humans too!
(hunch shoulders in fear)

The townspeople were all afraid.
(cower, shudder with teeth chattering)

They were afraid to step outside the city gate.
(wince, cautiously stick toe outside imaginary gate)

Then one day Francis came to town.
(walk in place, whistling)

He was sad to see the people so afraid.
(sad face)

He said, "*I'll* have a talk with that wolf!"
(point to self)

"Don't go, Brother Francis!" the people cried.
(shake head, reach out hands to hold him back)

"The wolf will gobble you up!"
(chomp, then smack lips)

But Francis trusted in God,
(point up to heaven)

the Master of ALL creation, even of wolves.
(make wide, sweeping gesture with both arms)

Francis took no weapon but the sign of the cross.
(make the sign of the cross)

Everyone followed behind to watch,
(tiptoe fearfully)

but they couldn't stand it.
(cover eyes in fear)

"We're afraid, Brother Francis!" they cried.
(cower, shiver, shake)

He told them, "You can stay *here*."
(point "here")

"I'll go *there* where the wolf lives."
(point "there")

Just then the wolf came charging...
(gallop in place, looking ferocious)

His jaws were open, showing his fangs.
(bare upper teeth, snarl)

He was heading straight toward Francis!
(point straight ahead)

Francis made the sign of the cross toward the wolf.
(make the sign of the cross)

The wolf stopped immediately.
(screech to a halt)

He snapped his jaws shut.
(snap jaws together tightly)

Francis scolded him, "Brother Wolf, you've been *bad!*"
(shake finger as in "naughty, naughty")

Brother Wolf lowered his head.
(lower head)

"You've gobbled up *people!*"
(shake finger)

Brother Wolf drooped his tail.
(make "tail" with hand behind you, then lower it)

"In Jesus' name, I tell you never to harm anyone again!"
(shake finger)

"Will you agree to that, Brother Wolf?"
(nod head, questioningly)

Brother Wolf looked up at Francis.
(look up, sideways)

He thumped his tail.
(thump "tail")

He wiggled his ears.
(grab ears and wiggle them manually)

Everyone knew he was saying "Yes."
(nod head vigorously)

"We know you're *hungry*, Brother Wolf," said Francis.
(rub tummy)

"The people will give you something to eat."
(eating motions)

"Every day they'll give you something to eat."
(eat faster)

"So make peace, Brother Wolf, the peace of the Lord,"
(hold out hand to shake)

"Will you shake paws with me?"
(shake "paws" up and down)

Brother Wolf walked back to town with Francis.
(walk in place, wag "tail" now and then)

The townspeople all cheered.
(cheer)

But Francis said, "Wait!"
(hold up hands in "halt" position)

"Look at this wolf," he said.
(point to "wolf")

"Every time you see Brother Wolf, remember,"
(tap temple)

"A wolf can eat up your body, it's true,"
(gobbling motions)

"But sin can eat up your soul!"
(more gobbling motions)

"Make peace with the wolf in your *town*,"
(shake "paws")

"And make peace with the wolf in your *heart*."
(place hand over heart)

The people heard his words.
(cup one hand behind ear)

They reached out and petted Brother Wolf.
(extend arm and pet, gingerly)

They reached out and made peace with one another.
(shake hands all around)

Every day they gave food to Brother Wolf.
(eating motions)

**Every day he walked around peaceful-
ly.**
(walk in place)

He licked the children's hands.
(licking motions)

He gave them rides on his back.
(bend over and pat back)

Brother Wolf never hurt anyone again.
(shake head from side to side)

And no one ever hurt *him*.
(shake head from side to side)

The dogs never barked at him anymore.
(whisper "woof, woof")

Fear had vanished away.
(hold open hands together, then blow on them, to signify something blowing away)

Brother Wolf grew old in their town.
(limp along slowly)

When he died, the people were sad.
(sad face)

The wolf of Gubbio had taught them peace.
(hold up fingers in "V" for peace sign)

There was peace in their *town*.
(shake hands in sign of peace with those near you)

And peace in their *hearts*.
(pat heart)

Peace in their *hearts*.
(pat heart more firmly)

And peace in their *town*.
(shake hands with everyone in the room if time permits)

Questions for Discussion

Call the students to order and ask them to sit down so they can talk about the following questions:

• What animal do you think is the scariest in the whole world? Can you imagine St. Francis calling that animal "brother" or "sister"? What would Francis say?

• How many parts of creation can you name as "brother" or "sister"? (sun, moon, trees, birds, flowers, rocks, rivers, oceans...)

• Can you think of ways to "make peace" with these "sisters" and "brothers" in creation?

- Can you think of ways to "make peace" in your town and in your heart?

- Does your parish have a "Blessing of the Animals" in honor of St. Francis' feast day? Would you like to take your pet to be blessed?

Closing Prayer

Thank you, Father, for giving us St. Francis as an example of how to love animals and birds, and how to be little "brothers" and "sisters" to all creation. Open our eyes to see the beauty that surrounds us on our planet earth and help us be good stewards of all that you have given us. Teach us to be peacemakers, starting right now and right here, and continuing every day of our lives. Amen.

Why Jack-o'-Lantern Wasn't a Saint

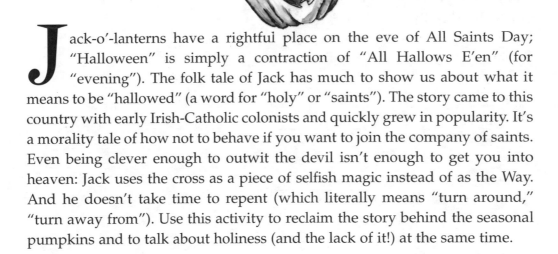

Jack-o'-lanterns have a rightful place on the eve of All Saints Day; "Halloween" is simply a contraction of "All Hallows E'en" (for "evening"). The folk tale of Jack has much to show us about what it means to be "hallowed" (a word for "holy" or "saints"). The story came to this country with early Irish-Catholic colonists and quickly grew in popularity. It's a morality tale of how not to behave if you want to join the company of saints. Even being clever enough to outwit the devil isn't enough to get you into heaven: Jack uses the cross as a piece of selfish magic instead of as the Way. And he doesn't take time to repent (which literally means "turn around," "turn away from"). Use this activity to reclaim the story behind the seasonal pumpkins and to talk about holiness (and the lack of it!) at the same time.

Once upon a time,
(twirl forefinger as if spinning a tale)

there was a little boy named Jack.
(measure "so high")

He was really, really smart.
(tap forehead several times)

But he was really, really lazy.
(pat mouth as if bored and yawn)

And so selfish...
(grab "things" against chest as if to say "mine!")

He never did *one* kind thing for anybody, *ever*.
(wag finger, shake head)

He used all those good brains
(tap forehead)

to get out of work.
(sneak off, tiptoeing)

The years rolled on and on,
("rolling" motions: rotate one forearm over the other)

but Jack never changed his ways.
(shake head sadly)

"I have plenty of time," he said,
(tap "wristwatch")

"to repent."
(turn 180 degrees)

All day long he lazed around town.
(yawn, pat mouth as if bored)

All night long he drank brew at the bar.
(pretend to drink)

Then one Halloween it came time for him to die.
(droop head, close eyes)

And UP jumped the devil to take him!
(stoop down, then jump up with hands like claws, snarl)

"You're mine!" said the devil.
(tap chest repeatedly and proudly)

Jack just yawned and scratched his head.
(yawn, scratch head as if unconcerned)

But his mind moved fast.
(tap-tap-tap on forehead)

"If you're really the devil," said Jack,
(point to "devil" offstage)

"change yourself into a dollar"
(rub fingers as in "money, money")

"so we don't have to pay the tab."
(shake head, conniving)

Now, the devil LOVES cheating.
(rub hands together fiendishly)

So, POOF! He disappeared.
(clap hands once, with upward motion as you say "POOF!")

A dollar lay on the bar.
(point down to "bar" in amazement)

Jack snatched it up, quick as a wink.
(grab "dollar" in fist)

His hand had a cross-shaped scar.
(trace cross on outside of fist)

"Let me out!" cried the devil.
(muffle the sound with both hands over mouth)

He was trapped by the power of the cross.
(trace cross on outside of fist)

"Give me a year to change my ways," said Jack.
(hold up fist with "devil" inside, addressing it firmly)

The devil said, "I promise."
(muffle the sound with both hands over mouth)

So Jack set him loose
(turn fist up, open it wide)

and went back to drinking his brew.
(quaff beer to finish)

He said, "I have plenty of time "
(tap "wristwatch")

"to repent."
(turn 180 degrees)

Another **year rolled around.**
("rolling" motions: rotate one forearm over the other)

Jack was gambling the next Halloween...
(pretend to throw dice)

when UP jumped the devil to take him.
(stoop down, then jump up with hands like claws, snarl)

Now Jack was clever...
(tap forehead)

He had whittled two dice
(hold up two fingers)

and fixed them so he could cheat.
(pretend to throw dice, then "Aha!")

"Looks like you caught me," said Jack.
(address "devil," yawn, pat mouth as if unconcerned)

"But let's roll for it, shall we?"
(mime rolling dice in hands)

Now, the devil LOVES dice.
(rub hands together, fiendishly)

They obey his every command.
(snap fingers twice: "Hut! Hut!")

"If *you* win, I'll go," said Jack.
(point to "you")

"If *I* win, I get one more year."
(hold up one finger)

So the devil rolled first.
(rub hands together, pretend to spit on them, roll)

"Snake Eyes! I win!" he said.
(point to eyes)

"My turn to try," said Jack.
(rub hands together, pretend to spit on them, roll)

His dice formed a cross
(make a "T" with hands)

with two threes.
(hold up three fingers on each hand)

"I've been tricked," yelled the devil,
(slap thigh angrily)

and stomped out of sight.
(turn to side, stomp, growl)

"Now I've plenty of time," said Jack,
(tap "wristwatch")

"to repent."
(turn 180 degrees)

But to his surprise,
(slap both hands on cheeks)

he died too soon.
(droop head, close eyes)

And went up to heaven's gate,
(point up)

where Saint Peter said, "No!"
(shake head sadly)

So Jack went "down there,"
(point down, fearfully)

where he got another surprise.
(slap cheeks with both hands)

The devil also said, "NO!"
(shake head angrily, fold arms on chest, adamant)

"Where will I go?" said Jack.
(shrug shoulders, look bewildered)

The devil snarled.
(snarl, hold hands up like claws)

"You're doomed to roam forever!"
(turn to side and trudge in place)

"But how will I see?" said Jack.
(cup hands at sides of eyes to attempt seeing)

"Take this coal," said the devil,
(reach down, pick up "coal" like a hot potato)

"and that pumpkin for a lantern."
(point down to an imaginary pumpkin)

Time had run out for Jack.
(tap "wristwatch," shake it, hold up to ear to listen)

There was no more time to repent.
(turn 180 degrees)

So when Halloween rolls around each year,
("rolling" motions: rotate one forearm over the other)

and we carve our jack-o'-lanterns,
(make carving motions on imaginary pumpkin)

we remember that Jack wasn't so *smart.*
(tap forehead, shake head)

He didn't get to *heaven* with the saints,
(point to heaven)

because he didn't take time to *repent.*
(turn 180 degrees)

He didn't get to *heaven* with the saints,
(point to heaven)

because he didn't take time to *repent.*
(turn 180 degrees)

Questions for Discussion

Take time to explain what "repent" means and that "Jack" is not a historical figure, by using questions like these:

• Is this a "real" story or a just-pretend story?

• If you could talk to Jack, what would you tell him?

• What are some ways people can "turn around" or "repent" from being selfish? From being lazy?

• Do you think it gets harder to change a bad habit if you wait till later to do it? How do you feel when you try to change a bad habit?

• What do we call people who *do* change their ways, to live as God calls them to live?

Closing Prayer

Lord, help us use Halloween as a time to think about what it means to be a saint. Inspire us to change our bad habits as quickly as we can, and remind us never to put off until tomorrow the kindness we can do for someone today. Keep us from harm as we have fun on Halloween, and help us tell others the reason why we make jack-o'-lanterns out of pumpkins on the Eve of All Saints Day. Amen.

Happy Feast Day, All You Saints!

November 1st is All Saints Day...and our feast day too. We tend to put the saints on pedestals and forget that we are all "called to holiness," which is what the word "saint" means. In the early church all the faithful were called "saints" simply because they had entered into a fervent relationship with Jesus. Later, people who modeled heroic virtue were venerated as saints by grass-roots acclaim. It was not until the 12th century that the process we know as canonization took hold, and along with it the "pedestalization" we're all familiar with. So we need to emphasize that even the canonized saints were not sinless or without human faults. What enables each one of us to be included in "When the Saints Go Marching In" is a deep desire to do God's will and a passionate love for all God's people.

Happy feast day, all you saints!
(point to everyone in room)

God wants *everybody* to be a saint.
(stretch arms wide to include everyone)

And that means *you* and *me*.
(point to others, then tap chest proudly)

The saints in heaven weren't so different from us.
(point to heaven, shaking head)

St. Peter was a fisherman
(cast out "fishing line" and then reel in a fish)

when he was called to follow Jesus.
(make beckoning sign with finger)

Sometimes Peter was *not* very saintly.
(shake head disapprovingly)

***Three* times he denied Jesus.**
(hold up three fingers)

But he repented quickly.
(cross yourself humbly as if making confession)

One time Peter tried to walk on water.
(tiptoe across "water" looking down fearfully)

And he started to s-i-i-i-n-k...
(sink down slowly, let voice taper off)

until Jesus lifted him up again.
(reach up hand to invisible Jesus, rise slowly)

Jesus told Peter he was a *rock*,
(put one fist on other as in "scissors, paper, rock" game)

and he helped Peter be a saint.
(draw halo above your head)

God wants *everybody* to be a saint.
(stretch arms wide to include everyone)

And that means *you* and *me*.
(point to others, then tap chest proudly)

St. Martha was a homemaker
(scrub floors on hands and knees, or dust fussily)

when she was called to follow Jesus.
(make beckoning motion with finger)

She loved to welcome Jesus for a visit
(gesture as if to say "Come in!")

and feed him dinner.
(make eating motions)

But Martha wasn't perfect...
(shake head)

Jesus had to scold her for being too fussy.
(shake finger, but smile)

But he helped her be a great saint.
(draw halo above your head)

God wants *everybody* to be a saint.
(stretch arms wide to include everyone)

And that means *you* and *me*.
(point to others, then tap chest proudly)

St. Francis was a rich kid
(rub fingers together as in "Money, money!")

when he was called to follow Jesus.
(make beckoning sign with finger)

Francis loved fancy clothes.
(smooth, arrange, and admire your clothes)

And lots of parties.
(pretend to dance with a partner)

And singing love songs.
(pretend to sing grand opera, mouth wide, hand sweeping)

But one day when Francis was praying,
(fold hands, bow head)

he heard God say, "Rebuild my Church!"
(cup ear to listen)

So Francis gave away all his fancy clothes,
(pretend to start taking off clothes)

put on a simple robe,
(pull "robe" over head, put arms through "sleeves")

and tied a rope for his belt.
(tie "rope" around waist)

Francis started preaching about God's love.
(make orator's gestures)

He even preached to the birds.
(lock thumbs, flutter fingers like wings)

God helped him be a great saint.
(draw halo above your head)

God wants *everybody* to be a saint.
(stretch arms wide to include everyone)

And that means *you* and *me*.
(point to others, then tap chest proudly)

St. Teresa of Avila liked to dance
(snap fingers like castanets, do a "flamenco")

when she was called to follow Jesus.
(make beckoning sign with finger)

She walked hundreds of miles
(trudge in place)

all around Spain
(sweep hands in circle)

and founded new convents of nuns.
(fold hands, bow head, be demure)

One time she was riding a mule,
(gallop in place)

and she fell off in the mud,
(fall down, wipe "mud" from arms and skirts)

and she complained to Jesus in heaven.
(shake fist at sky)

But Jesus didn't mind.
(shake head)

He helped Teresa be a great saint.
(draw halo above your head)

God wants *everybody* to be a saint.
(stretch arms wide to include everyone)

And that means *you* and *me*.
(point to others, then tap chest proudly)

Mother Teresa of Calcutta was a teeny, tiny nun.
(extend palm downward to measure "so high")

And God helped her be a great saint.
(draw halo above your head)

Every morning she prayed at least an hour.
(fold hands in prayer)

Then she walked the streets of the cities
(walk in place, looking around)

and found all the people nobody wants...
(shake your head sadly)

because they're sick...
(droop your body, wipe your "feverish" brow)

or dying...
(drop head on chest, close eyes)

or too poor.
(turn imaginary pockets inside out)

Mother Teresa carried them gently home...
(lift and carry imaginary person)

and washed off all the dirt...
(wash face and arms gently)

and gave them medicine...
(pour medicine in "spoon"; give it to yourself)

and covered them nice and warm.
(wrap imaginary blanket around yourself)

They all received God's love
(hands over heart)

from teeny, tiny Mother Teresa.
(extend palm downward to measure "so high")

God wants *everybody* to be a saint.
(stretch arms wide to include everyone)

And that means *you* and *me*.
(point to others, then tap chest proudly)

My name is Saint (N.).
(point to self and say your name; tell others to name themselves)

I probably won't ever walk on water,
(tiptoe fearfully, like St. Peter)

or ride a donkey in Spain,
(gallop in place like Teresa of Avila)

but God is helping *me* be a saint too.
(draw halo above your head)

I'm just an ordinary person.
(shrug shoulders)

I wake up s-l-o-w-l-y every morning,
(stretch, rub eyes, yawn)

and I pray to God to help me do my best.
(fold hands in prayer)

I like to laugh...
(turn corners of mouth up with fingers)

and sing...
(pretend to be opera singer)

and work.
(hammer one fist on the other)

Sometimes I get mad...
(hands on hips, scowl)

and sometimes I cry...
(rub eyes, sob)

But God loves me anyway.
(hands over heart)

He wants me to be a saint *anyway.*
(draw halo around and above your head)

God wants *everybody* **to be a saint.**
(stretch arms wide to include everyone)

And that means *you* **and** *me.*
(point to others, then tap chest proudly)

GOD WANTS EVERYBODY TO BE A SAINT!
(shout this line)

So happy feast day, all you saints!
(point to everyone in room)

(To end this echo pantomime, the teacher can repeat the last line more and more soft-ly, till it ends with silent mouthing of the words. Or, he or she can move among all the students individually saying "Happy Feast Day, St. Billy," calling them each by name, while students circulate doing the same thing.)

Questions for Discussion

Continue your emphasis on what it means to be a saint with some of the fol-lowing questions:

- Who is your favorite saint? Is he or she ever shown carrying something as a symbol?
- Do you know anything about the saint you're named for? Who can you ask?
- Catholics don't worship the saints, but we do honor them and ask them to pray for us. Do you know what the word "intercede" means? Is it possible to "intercede" for others while you're still alive?
- Can you imagine yourself as a "patron saint" of something you're good at doing? What would it be, and what would you want as your symbol?
- Pope John Paul II has canonized lots of new saints; where can you find out about a new one?

Closing Prayer

All you saints in heaven, pray for those of us still here on earth. Ask God to give us the graces we need to bring the love of Jesus into our work and into our play. Help us learn more saint stories so we can be inspired to grow in holiness and to work hard at whatever things the Lord sets before us. We look forward to the day when all of us will be rejoicing together in heaven. Amen.

Thanksgiving Is Knowing Who to Thank

In 1863 Abraham Lincoln established Thanksgiving as a national holiday, but New England and other parts of the country had been celebrating it for two centuries. Lincoln said our blessings "should be solemnly, reverently, and gratefully acknowledged with one heart and one voice." Gratitude and prayer have been the soul of the celebration from the beginning. Thanksgiving is an opportunity to teach not only about the love of religious freedom, courage, and resourcefulness of the original Pilgrims, but also that the word "pilgrim" itself is a religious term for someone who travels on a long journey to a holy destination. We are all "pilgrims" while we journey on earth toward heaven, and we all need to become more and more thankful for this grace.

Thanksgiving means *turkey*!
(tuck hands under armpits, flap like bird)

Thanksgiving means *pumpkin pie*!
(roll eyes, eat imaginary pie)

Thanksgiving means lots of good food!
(rub tummy, raise eyebrows several times)

But does Thanksgiving mean *prayer* anymore?
(fold hands in prayer, look questioningly, shrug)

Are we rich in food,
(make gobbling motions with mouth and hands)

but poor in thanks?
(mime turning pockets inside out, shrug)

The first Pilgrims knew who to thank.
(point to heaven)

They prayed as hard as they could.
(hunch shoulders earnestly, fold hands, squeeze eyes shut)

They were happy for the good harvest.
(turn corners of mouth up with forefingers)

There had been plenty of sunshine...
(raise arms in large circle to indicate sun)

and plenty of rain...
(imitate falling rain, with fingers fluttering down)

which meant plenty of food for the cold, cold winter.
(huddle, shiver, "Brrr, brrr")

And they knew who to thank!
(point to heaven)

They wanted to have a *big* feast
(throw arms out widely)

to give thanks to our good God.
(fold hands in prayer)

And to invite Squanto, their Native American friend.
(beckoning motions on "invite")

He was "a special instrument from God," they said.
(point to heaven)

Squanto had shown them how to find berries.
(pretend to pick berries and put in basket)

He showed them which plants were good to eat...
(make eating motions)

and which plants were poison.
(grasp neck with hands, stick tongue out of mouth, roll eyes)

He taught them about corn...
(mime eating corn on the cob)

and how to put a dead fish in with the seeds.
(hold nose and pretend to hold fish at arm's length)

What would they have done without Squanto?
(shake head in wonder, shrug)

Squanto ran to invite his chief.
(turn to side and run in place)

The Pilgrims cooked lots and lots of food.
(pretend to stir big cauldron)

Then Squanto came back with the chief.
(turn to opposite side, run in place)

But the Pilgrims were surprised!
(slap forehead, eyes wide with shock)

The chief had brought ninety of his braves!
(mime watching row after row of people pass by)

They were all covered with bear grease.
(slather arms and shoulders with "grease" like suntan lotion)

Would there be enough food for ninety more people?
(shrug shoulders, turn hands upward)

"Don't worry!" said the chief.
(shake head and smile)

He sent his braves off with bows and arrows.
(mime pulling arrow from quiver and drawing bow)

They brought back *five* deer.
(hold up five fingers)

There was plenty of food for the feast.
(rub tummy, smile)

The oldest Pilgrim prayed a prayer of thanks.
(fold hands, bow head)

He knew who to thank!
(point to heaven)

And then the feasting began.
(eating motions, slow, then faster and faster)

The first Thanksgiving lasted *three* days.
(hold up three fingers)

The Pilgrims and Indians prayed a lot...
(fold hands, bow head)

and they ate a lot...
(eating motions, then hold tummy as if overstuffed)

and they had races and other games.
(run in place)

The first Pilgrims knew who to thank.
(point to heaven)

But most of us don't remember.
(shake head)

We're too busy eating...
(eating motions)

and watching TV.
(lean head on fists and gaze fixedly at a "TV")

We're rich in blessings...
(point to clothing, jewelry, the whole room)

but poor in thanks.
(turn pockets inside out, shrug)

How do we say "thanks" to God?
(shrug shoulders, turn hands upward)

Some churches bring food baskets to the poor,
(turn to side, walk in place, carrying basket of food)

or cook a special meal in the soup kitchen.
(stir a big "cauldron")

Those are good ways to say "thanks" to God,
(point to heaven)

by sharing our blessings with others,
(mime handing out things from a "basket" on arm)

just like Jesus told us in the Bible:
(open hands together as if reading from book)

"Whatever you do to the least of these,"
(point to people all around you)

"you do to me."
(point to self)

This kind of "thanks-giving" we need *all year long!*
(spread hands wide, expansively)

Sometimes there's a prayer service at Thanksgiving...
(fold hands in prayer)

different churches all praying together as one.
(hold up one finger)

That's another good way to say "thanks" to the Lord,
(point to heaven)

because Jesus prayed that we all might be one.
(sweep arm inclusively)

Just as he and the Father are one.
(point to self then up to heaven)

So remember those interchurch prayer services
(tap temple with forefinger)

when you want to give thanks to God.
(fold hands in prayer)

Some people go to Mass on Thanksgiving.
(turn to side, walk in place)

That's a *special* way to say "Thanks" to God,
(lift up open hand to heaven)

because "Eucharist" means "Thank you."
(hold up arms in praise)

Every time we go to Mass, we know who to thank!
(point to heaven)

How can *you* be rich in thanks?
(point to those in group)

You can do any of these things,
(sweep arm inclusively)

or even make up your *own* traditions.
(tap chest assertively)

So when you see fall colors like orange and brown,
(peer around, shielding eyes with hand)

and decorations like corn stalks and Indian corn,
(point around room to imaginary corn stalks)

***think* "Thanks!"**
(tap temple with one finger)

"Thank you" to God!
(point to heaven)

"Thank you" to everybody!
(sweep arm in circle)

Put the "Thanks" in Thanksgiving!
(start applause, as in "Let's hear it for Thanksgiving")

Because we *know* who to thank!
(point to heaven)

We *know* who to thank!
(speak more softly, point to heaven more emphatically)

Questions for Discussion

Seat the children comfortably and then begin the discussion.

- What's your favorite food at Thanksgiving? Do you say thank you to those who cooked the big dinner? Do you remember to say thank you for dinners on ordinary days too?

- What relatives do you see at Thanksgiving? Do you remember to thank them for the things they do for you?

- Does your family say a special grace before dinner? How do you feel when you're asked to pray in front of relatives?

- Make a list of things you're thankful for. Before you go to sleep tonight, read this list and talk to God about it.

- What way can your family help the poor this Thanksgiving?

Closing Prayer

We thank you, good and generous God, for all the blessings you've lavished on us and on our country. Don't ever let us forget who to thank. Help us make this a blessed and prayerful Thanksgiving. Amen.

Also make sure the children know the traditional prayers for Grace Before Meals ("Bless us, O Lord, and these your gifts, which we are about to receive from your bounty, through Christ our Lord. Amen."), and the one which is more difficult to form into a habit, the Grace After Meals ("We give you thanks, Almighty God, for these and all the benefits we have received from your goodness, through Christ our Lord. Amen.").

Have a Maranatha Advent

The first Sunday of Advent begins the new liturgical year as well as our preparation for celebrating the birth of Jesus. "Advent" means "the coming," so the church uses this season to also prepare us for Jesus' second coming which could be at any hour, on any day. The early church ended all its liturgies with "Maranatha," expecting that the second coming would be in their lifetime. The idea of the "middle coming" of Christ originated with St. Bernard of Clairvaux (1090–1153). He says that at the Lord's first coming, he came in our flesh and our weakness, and in his final coming he will come in glory and majesty. His "middle coming" lies between the other two and is hidden and private: he comes to the individual soul in spirit and power, to be like a road on which we travel from the first coming to the last. It's an engaging thought to begin the new church year.

"Maranatha" is such a *long* word...
(lower voice on "long," measure with hands, stretching it out)

But all it means is "Come, Lord."
(beckon)

We hear it a lot during Advent.
(cup ear to hear)

Advent is a special time each year.
(tap "wristwatch")

It's a time to learn about hope.
(cross fingers, squint eyes shut, tilt head up hopefully)

Especially hoping in the Lord.
(point up to heaven)

It's a time to learn how to wait.
(fold arms, tap foot impatiently, roll eyes)

Especially waiting for the Lord.
(point up to heaven)

It's a time to learn about joy.
(turn up corners of mouth with fingers: happy face)

Especially rejoicing in the Lord.
(point up to heaven)

And it's a time to turn away from all our sins.
(turn around 180 degrees)

So we pray "Maranatha,"
(praying hands)

which means, "Come, Lord."
(beckon vigorously)

In Advent we can hardly wait for the Lord to come!
(tap foot, look at watch)

We want Christmas to hurry up.
(beckon impatiently, insistently)

We run around getting things ready...
(run in place)

with presents to wrap...
(mime tying a bow on a present)

cookies to make...
(stir "batter" in bowl)

Christmas cards to write...
(write "cards")

And we pray, "Maranatha."
(praying hands)

"Come, Lord!"
(beckon vigorously)

But there are *three* comings of Jesus we wait for.
(hold up three fingers)

The first is Jesus coming as a baby.
(rock "baby" in arms)

That's the "coming" most of us think of:
(tap forehead)

when there was no room in the inn...
(shake head sadly)

and angels appeared to the shepherds...
(flap arms as wings)

and the glory of the Lord shone round about them...
(raise arms, flutter fingers in arc down to each side)

and the wise men came riding camels.
(gallop in place)

And for that we pray, "Maranatha,"
(praying hands)

which means, "Come, Lord!"
(beckon vigorously)

But we also pray for the *Second* Coming of Jesus,
(hold up two fingers)

when he comes again in glory.
(raise arms, flutter fingers in arc to each side)

We don't know the day or the hour.
(tap "wristwatch," shake head)

Only the Father in heaven knows that.
(point to heaven)

Our job is to be ready and stay alert...
(perk up; blink eyes; hold eyelids open)

and to keep busy building God's kingdom...
(tap one fist on top of other: "building")

and to make sure we're at peace with each other...
(shake hands with several in "sign of peace")

so when Jesus comes at the end of time...
(tap "wristwatch," then cover it up)

he'll find us busy building the kingdom.
(tap one fist on top of other more assertively)

So for the Second Coming we pray, "Maranatha,"
(praying hands)

which means, "Come, Lord!"
(beckon vigorously)

The *third* coming is the "Middle Coming" of Jesus.
(hold up three fingers)

It's for each person privately...
(tap chest)

when Jesus comes into our heart.
(hold hands over heart)

He waits to be invited in.
(beckon, "Come on in")

He stands outside knocking.
(knock on "door")

And we open the door of our heart to him.
(put hands over heart, then "open" as a door)

We say "Yes," and he comes in.
(nod, and close "doors" of heart over him)

Jesus becomes King in our hearts.
(place imaginary crown on head)

How do we get ready for his "Middle Coming"?
(shrug shoulders, turn palms up)

We pray to make our hearts ready for him.
(praying hands)

We go to church cheerfully.
(walk bouncily in place, smile)

We do good deeds in secret.
(tiptoe stealthily, looking over shoulder)

We steer clear of bad things.
(turn head aside, push away with palms)

So, for his "personal coming," we pray "Maranatha,"
(praying hands)

which means, "Come, Lord!"
(beckon vigorously)

"Maranatha" is a *long Aramaic* word.
(measure long word with hands)

That's the language Jesus spoke.
(flap thumb against fingers in "talking" sign)

So we're asking him in his own language...
(point to heaven)

"Come, Lord!"
(beckon vigorously)

"Come, Lord Jesus."
(beckon even more vigorously)

"Won't you please, please come, Lord?"
(praying hands, begging and pleading)

So, have a Maranatha Advent, everybody!
(gesture around to everyone)

Amen, amen, come Lord Jesus!
(raise hands up, praising and welcoming)

Questions for Discussion

Let the children be seated and talk about what Advent means to them:

- What kinds of Advent calendars have you seen? How do they help make each day count?

- Do you know anyone who is very patient? How do they act that lets you know they have patience? How do you feel when people are impatient with you?

- If you stay busy while you wait for something, does time seem to go faster? Give some examples.

- What are you doing to get ready for Christmas? How are you "getting your heart" ready?

- Is there anything special you can do to bring peace to others during Advent?

Closing Prayer

Lord, open our hearts to welcome you with joy this season. Keep us from getting too caught up in the commercial side of Christmas, and take away anything that would separate us from you. Show us how we can bring hope and peace to those around us during this busy season. Amen.

John the Baptist
Ate Grasshoppers

The figure of John the Baptist looms doubly large in the gospels: he's the last of the Old Testament prophets and at the same time the New Testament's herald of the Messiah. John has two feast days on the liturgical calendar, the day of his birth (June 24th) and the day of his beheading (August 29th), but we usually associate him with Advent because of the inspiration of his message. Baptism was practiced by other preachers and other sects before John's time, he was not the first—or the last—to baptize in the River Jordan. The famous story of John's birth to Zachary and Elizabeth (Luke 1) is not included in this echo pantomime, but part of it is told in "Mary's Story."

John the Baptist lived *way* out in the desert.
(indicate "way" out, pointing "offstage")

He was a cousin of Jesus.
(hold up forefingers next to each other to show closeness)

He was a voice crying in the wilderness.
(cup hands like megaphone around mouth)

"Prepare the way of the Lord," he said.
(imitate breaststroke, as if "plowing through")

"Turn away from your sins!"
(turn 180 degrees around, fold arms across chest)

John wore a camel hair tunic.
(look self over, brush off "tunic," scratch)

And he ate grasshoppers
(catch "grasshopper" and pop into mouth)

and wild honey.
(spoon "honey" into mouth, lick lips: "mmm")

People came from all around to hear him preach.
(sweeping motions for "all around")

He baptized them in the River Jordan.
(pour "water" over imaginary heads)

Hundreds and hundreds of people came.
(beckon "people" from all directions)

"Prepare the way of the Lord," he said.
(imitate breaststroke, as if "plowing through")

"Turn away from your sins!"
(turn 180 degrees around, fold arms across chest)

"Share your food with those who have none!"
(dole out "food" from "basket")

"If you have two coats in your closet, give away one!"
(hold up two fingers, then one)

More and more people came.
(beckon more people in, from all directions)

And John kept baptizing.
(pour water over imaginary heads)

"Someone is coming, greater than I," he said.
(point to self)

"I am not worthy to untie his sandals."
(stoop to untie "sandals")

"So turn away from your sins."
(turn 180 degrees around, fold arms across chest)

One day he saw Jesus coming to the River Jordan.
(shade eyes, looking in distance)

"Behold the Lamb of God," he said.
(point offstage)

Jesus walked up to be baptized.
(walk briskly in place)

"*You* should be baptizing *me*!" John said.
(point: "you" and "me")

But he baptized Jesus as he was told,
(humbly pour water over imaginary head)

and the sky opened up.
(look up, lift arms up together, spread hands open)

A dove came down,
(lock thumbs and flutter fingers down like wings)

and a voice came from heaven:
(cup hands like megaphone around mouth)

"This is my beloved son,"
(speak through megaphone)

"in whom I am well pleased."
(continue to speak through megaphone)

John felt humble.
(bow from waist in humility)

"He must increase, I must decrease," he said.
(two hands: one going higher, then the other going lower)

Some disciples left and followed Jesus.
(turn right abruptly, trot in place)

Then King Herod marched John off to prison.
(turn left abruptly, march, hands behind back, head bowed)

John said the king was wrong to marry his brother's wife.
(shake head and shake forefinger)

So Herod's wife got mad at John the Baptist.
(scowl, shake fist)

So mad she wanted him dead.
(slit throat with finger, close eyes)

But John's friends came to prison to see him.
(run in place)

They told him everything Jesus was doing.
(with thumb and fingers, indicate "talking")

John thought and thought about these things.
(adopt "The Thinker" pose)

He sent his friends to ask Jesus,
(shoo the "friends" off)

"Are you the one who is to come?"
(shrug shoulders, spread hands outward)

Jesus sent the friends back, saying,
(shoo the "friends" off in opposite direction)

"Tell John you've seen the lame walk,"
(limp painfully, then straighten up and walk proudly)

"and the blind see,"
(place hands over eyes, then remove abruptly)

"and the deaf hear."
(place hands over ears, then remove abruptly)

Back in prison, this satisfied John.
(nod head, satisfied)

Then King Herod had a birthday party.
(stoop to blow out imaginary candles)

There was lots of feasting
(make eating motions, then gobble)

and lots of drinking.
(make drinking motions, then get tipsy)

Herod's stepdaughter Salome danced.
(imitate a hula or a belly dance)

Salome danced so beautifully,
(continue dancing)

that King Herod was delighted.
(clap hands vigorously)

He promised her anything she wanted.
(sweep hands in a horizontal "X" on "anything")

Salome ran to ask her mother what to ask for.
(turn to right, run in place)

"John the Baptist's head!" her mother said.
(snarl, slit throat with finger)

"On a platter, and right NOW!"
(snap fingers twice on "now")

Salome ran back to King Herod.
(turn to left, run in place)

She asked for John the Baptist's head
(slit throat with finger)

on a platter, and right NOW.
(snap fingers twice on "now")

King Herod's soldiers marched off.
(turn to right and march)

And came back with John the Baptist's head.
(turn to left, march back holding "platter" like a waiter)

Salome took John's head to her mother.
(take "platter," hold far out from body, avert eyes, make face)

And John's friends buried his body.
(make digging motions)

They ran to tell Jesus.
(run in place)

"No one born of woman was greater," said Jesus.
(shake head sadly)

Today we remember John the Baptist,
(tap forehead)

especially his words: "Prepare the way of the Lord!"
(imitate breaststroke, as if "plowing through")

And, "Turn away from your sins!"
(turn 180 degrees around, fold arms across chest)

We thank God for sending John the Baptist.
(point to heaven)

We're glad he was a "voice crying in the wilderness."
(cup hands like megaphone around mouth)

We pray for *strength* to do what he said.
(flex muscles in both arms)

It's hard to "Prepare the way of the Lord."
(show effort with breaststroke)

It's hard to "turn away from our sins."
(turn slowly around 180 degrees, fold arms across chest)

We need John to pray for us.
(fold hands in prayer)

And we need to pray for each other.
(spread arms inclusively)

"Prepare the way of the Lord!"
(do breaststroke, as if "plowing through")

"Prepare the way of the Lord."
(repeat final line several times, diminishing loudness)

Questions for Discussion

After the students have quieted down, let them talk about John the Baptist with starter questions like these:

- Have you ever been out in a desert? What's it like?

- How can you "prepare the way of the Lord" in everyday ways?

- Do you share your food and clothing with "those who have none"? Does the parish have a way to do this?

- In what ways can you help each other "turn away" from doing wrong?

- Have you ever asked your parents to tell you about the day of your baptism? Did you cry when the water was poured over your head?

Closing Prayer

Lord Jesus, we ask for the intercession of John the Baptist as we prepare for your coming. Give us the courage to turn away from temptation, and the patience to wait joyfully for you to fill our hearts. Don't let us be afraid to speak out against wrongdoing the way John the Baptist did. Teach us to understand more about our own baptism and about the ways we are called to help the blind to see and the deaf to hear. Amen.

St. Nicholas, the Generous Bishop

Teaching the distinctions between the fourth-century St. Nicholas and his red-suited counterpart can be a delicate business, especially with the very young. Yet it's worth the effort because modern advertising has switched the original message of charitable giving into materialistic "gimme." The real-life Nicholas was Bishop of Myra (southwestern Turkey), famous for his holiness, zeal, and legendary generosity. He died about 350 AD. The three bags of gold that Nicholas gave to a poor father to use as dowries for his daughters are the origin of the pawnbrokers' symbol of three gold balls. Nicholas' feast day is December 6th. Older children will easily see how "Santa" is a form of "Sanctus" (Saint), and "Claus" is a shortened form of Nicholas.

St. Nicholas lived a long time ago.
(jerk thumb repeatedly over shoulder on "ago")

But he was a real person like you and me.
(point to "you" and "me")

When he was still just a little boy,
(measure "so high" with hand)

his mother and father died.
(close eyes, droop head)

This made Nicholas very sad.
(pull down corners of mouth: sad face)

But it also gave him a love for children
(hands over heart)

that he never ever lost.
(shake head, keeping hands over heart)

His parents left him lots of money.
(rub fingers together for "money, money")

So he gave gifts to the poor,
(reach in pocket, hand out "money")

in Jesus' name.
(point up to heaven)

When Nicholas grew up,
(measure "so high," and steadily move taller)

he became a bishop.
(indicate a bishop's hat on top of head)

And he kept on giving gifts to the poor,
(reach in pocket, hand out "money")

in Jesus' name.
(point to heaven)

Once he heard about a man
(cup ear for "heard")

who had three daughters,
(hold up three fingers, tick off)

but no money for their dowry.
(rub fingers together for "money": shake head)

Girls needed a dowry to get married.
(mime putting a wedding ring on finger)

Nicholas heard the oldest daughter crying.
(rub eyes, pretend to weep)

She wanted to get married and couldn't.
(indicate ring finger and shake head)

So one night when everyone was asleep,
(pillow head on hands)

Nicholas tiptoed by the poor man's house,
(turn to the side, tiptoe, make "shhh" motions)

and threw a bag of gold over the wall,
(toss imaginary "bag," like basketball)

giving a gift in Jesus' name.
(point to heavens)

In the morning the daughter woke up,
(yawn, rub eyes, stretch)

and was so surprised!
(slap cheeks with hands)

A bag of gold was lying in the courtyard!
(point to "bag" on ground, amazed)

She ran off and got married right away.
(turn to the side, run briskly in place)

When the second daughter grew up,
(measure "so high," taller and taller)

she wanted to get married too.
(mime putting wedding ring on finger)

And she also cried and cried,
(rub eyes, weeping)

because her father still didn't have her dowry.
(rub fingers together for "money," shake head)

Nicholas waited till everyone was asleep,
(pillow head on hands)

and tiptoed by their house again,
(turn sideways, tiptoe, make "shhh" motions)

and threw *another* bag of gold over the wall,
(toss imaginary "bag," like basketball)

giving a gift in Jesus' name.
(point to heavens)

The second daughter was surprised too!
(slap cheeks with hands)

***Another* bag of gold was lying in the courtyard!**
(point to "bag" on ground, amazed)

So *she* ran off and got married right away.
(turn to side, run briskly in place)

When Nicholas heard that the *third* daughter
(hold up three fingers, tick off)

had grown up
(measure "so high," taller and taller)

and was old enough to get married,
(put "wedding ring" on finger)

he didn't wait another minute.
(shake head)

He tiptoed past their house at night,
(turn to side, tiptoe, make "shhh" motions)

and threw a *third* bag of gold over the wall,
(toss imaginary "bag" like basketball)

giving a gift in Jesus' name.
(point to heavens)

The third daughter was just as surprised as her sisters
(slap cheeks with hands)

to find a bag of gold in the courtyard.
(point to "bag" on ground, amazed)

The father knelt down on the spot,
(kneel down, awed)

and thanked God.
(bow head, clasp hands in fervent prayer)

The man and his daughters never knew
(stand up again, shake head)

that those three bags of gold
(hold up three fingers)

given in secret in the middle of the night
(turn to the side, tiptoe, make "shh" motions)

were the start of giving gifts in Jesus' name
(point to heavens)

on the feast of St. Nicholas.
(make imaginary Bishop's hat over head)

In some countries children set out their shoes,
(stick out foot and point to shoe)

and are surprised by gifts the next morning.
(slap cheeks in surprise)

In our country we hang up stockings,
(stick out foot, tug at sock)

and are surprised by gifts the next morning.
(slap cheeks in surprise)

Nicholas is the patron saint of children.
(indicate lots of "children," measuring "so high")

He wanted them to be happy.
(turn up corners of mouth with fingers)

Especially the children of the poor.
(pull "pockets" inside out, turn empty palms up, sad)

He didn't want to make children greedy.
(hunch over, hug "things" to self, make mean face)

He taught us to give our gifts
(hand out "gifts")

in Jesus' name.
(point to heavens)

To give our gifts,
(hand out "gifts")

in Jesus' name.
(point to heavens)

Questions for Discussion

Let the children sit down and check to see that they know what a "dowry" is before beginning.

- Do you plan to give someone a gift this Christmas that makes you excited? Is it a secret?

- Have you ever wanted to share and be generous because you saw someone else doing it first? What did you do and how did it make you feel?

- Are there more TV advertisements for toys during this season? Do you think this makes kids more greedy, or more generous?

- After Christmas, what would happen if you asked your friends, "What did you give," instead of "What did you get"?

Closing Prayer

Lord Jesus, let us be generous just like St. Nicholas was. Give us his love for the poor, and his energy and creativity to think of ways we can help them. Turn our thoughts to others, Lord, and stop us from thinking only about ourselves. Show us the way we too can "give gifts in Jesus' name." Amen.

Our Lady
of Guadalupe

Our Lady of Guadalupe is patroness of the Americas; her feast day is December 12th. The story of her appearance a few miles from Mexico City on a cold December morning in 1531, to a simple Aztec convert to Christianity, underscores God's constant love for the poor and the oppressed. The miraculous image on Juan Diego's *tilma* (poncho) still hangs above the altar of the basilica in Mexico City, venerated by an unending stream of pilgrims. It has not faded or peeled in all the years since it first astonished the Bishop. The black ribbon across Our Lady's abdomen was a sign of pregnancy for that culture, and so pro-lifers have recently made an effort to protect the unborn under her patronage.

Early one morning in Mexico,
(yawn, rub eyes)

Juan Diego was walking to church.
(walk in place)

He walked to the top of a hill.
(walk with more effort, lifting knees higher)

He heard beautiful music around him.
(cup ear to hear, look around)

"Am I in heaven?" he said.
(point up to heaven, raise eyebrows)

A beautiful Lady was there.
(smooth down clothes, fold hands, tilt head)

Juan Diego bowed before her.
(bow from the waist, courtly)

He listened as she spoke to him.
(cup ear to hear)

"I am Mary, the Virgin," she said.
(fold hands, bow head)

"I want you to build me a church,"
(lift imaginary stones to "build")

"so everyone will know my protection."
(sweeping gesture with arms to include "everyone")

"Go to the Bishop and tell him."
(point offstage)

Juan Diego bowed before her.
(bow from waist)

He hurried at once to the Bishop.
(run in place)

No one paid him any attention.
(put nose in air, tip shoulder in disdain)

Juan Diego was only a poor man.
(empty pockets)

He didn't know how to read and write.
(pretend to read, shake head)

So no one paid him any attention.
(put nose in air, tip shoulder in disdain)

Juan Diego waited and waited.
(tap foot, fold arms)

At last he talked to the Bishop.
(make "talking" gesture with hands)

The Bishop didn't know what to think,
(frown, tap temple)

so he sent him away.
("shoo" gesture of dismissal)

Juan Diego walked away sadly,
(walk in place, head down, sad face)

and slowly went back to the hilltop.
(slow down walking in place)

He bowed to the beautiful Lady.
(bow from waist)

"I did what you told me," he said.
(nod head, point to self)

"The Bishop didn't believe me."
(shake head sadly)

"I'm sorry I failed, my Lady..."
(shake head sadly, shrug)

"Send somebody better than me."
(hang head, shrug, hand on chest)

The Lady spoke to him gently.
(gesture with hand, as in "Wait a minute")

"*You* are the one that I want."
(point to "you")

"Go back to the Bishop again."
(point offstage)

"Tell him I'm Mary, the Mother of God."
(pat tummy, fold hands in prayer)

Juan Diego bowed before her.
(bow from waist)

And back to the Bishop he went.
(walk quickly in place)

Still no one paid him any attention.
(put nose in air, tip shoulder in disdain)

He waited and waited.
(tap foot, fold arms)

Finally he talked to the Bishop.
(make "talking" gesture with hands)

The Bishop listened this time.
(cup ear)

He told him to ask for a *sign*.
(raise folded hands up, beseeching)

Juan Diego bowed and said yes.
(bow from waist)

He hurried back to the Lady
(run in place)

and told her everything that happened.
(gesture animatedly, mouthing words)

She nodded and spoke once again.
(nod several times)

"Come back here tomorrow," she said.
(Point down to "here")

"I will give you the sign that he wants."
(raise folded hands up, beseeching)

Juan Diego ran to his house.
(run in place)

But he found that his uncle was sick.
(droop head, close eyes)

He needed to run for the doctor.
(run in place, head down)

He didn't go back to the hilltop.
(shake head, point offstage)

Then his uncle seemed to be dying,
(droop head, close eyes)

and Juan Diego ran for the priest.
(run in place, head down)

But there on the road was the Lady!
(run, then halt, look up in surprise)

"Do not be troubled," she said.
(gesture with hand, as in "Wait a minute")

"Your uncle is already well."
(droop then perk up, blink bright-eyed)

"I hold you close in my mantle."
(swoop arms as if enfolding in mantle)

"I hold you close in my love."
(fold hands over heart)

"Go to the place on the hilltop."
(point offstage to hilltop)

"Bring back the flowers you find."
(gathering gestures, as if picking flowers)

Juan Diego ran to the hilltop.
(run in place)

Roses covered the place.
(sweeping, inclusive gestures)

It wasn't the season for flowers.
(shake head)

It was cold and frozen December.
(shiver, teeth chattering)

Juan Diego picked lots of roses.
(gathering gestures, as if picking flowers)

He carried them in his tilma,
(pretend to fold into front of shirt or sweater)

which was like a cloak or a poncho.
(smooth out clothing as if wearing a poncho)

He took the roses to Our Lady.
(run in place, holding "tilma" folded)

"Go to the Bishop," she said.
(point offstage)

"Show them to no one but him."
(shake head)

Juan Diego ran back to the Bishop.
(run in place, holding "tilma" up)

He unfolded the tilma to show him.
(let down the fold of the "tilma")

The roses fell to the ground.
(sweeping gesture, all around)

The Bishop fell to his knees.
(kneel down, hands folded, awestruck)

His eyes stared at the tilma.
(stay kneeling, pry eyes open with fingers)

Juan Diego looked at his tilma.
(stand up, twist head, look down at clothes)

A picture was there of the Lady.
(fold hands in prayer, tilt head)

The Bishop prayed and gave thanks.
(bow head, hands crossed over chest)

He carried the tilma to his chapel.
(hold up "tilma," walk in place)

The people heard of the picture.
(cup ears)

They walked miles to see it.
(trudge in place)

They heard of Our Lady's protection...
(fold hands in prayer, tilt head)

that she folded them *all* in her mantle...
(swoop arms as if enfolding all in mantle)

that she held them *all* in her love.
(fold hands over heart)

You can still see Our Lady's picture
(shade eyes as if looking)

on the tilma, near Mexico City.
(hold up "tilma")

Even today she holds us,
(fold hands over heart)

and enfolds us *all* in her mantle.
(swoop arms as if enfolding all in mantle)

We pray she will always protect us.
(raise folded hands, beseeching)

Our Lady of Guadalupe, pray for us.
(fold hands, tilt head)
(repeat two more times, quietly)

Questions for Discussion

If possible, show a picture of Our Lady of Guadalupe or a map of the Americas as you lead the discussion. Also, make sure the children know that a "tilma" is like a poncho.

- Have you ever been to Mexico? Can you find Mexico City on the map?

- Does anyone in your family grow roses? When do roses usually bloom?

- How did Our Lady show she understood that Juan Diego needed to take care of his uncle first?

- Why do you think people ignored a poor Indian like Juan Diego?

- How can we show we won't "ignore" people who are poor, or different, or uneducated?

Closing Prayer

Our Lady of Guadalupe, pray for all of us, especially those of us in North and South America. Ask your son, our Lord, to bring us closer together and to give us more respect for each other. Keep showing us the value of each human life. Wrap your mantle of protection around the poor and the unborn and show us ways we can help them, and ways to help those who can't read or write. We ask this in the name of Jesus, Lord and Brother of us all. Amen.

Mary's Story

Mary's humility and her sense of wonder at being chosen to be Mother of Jesus is not limited to the Annunciation or to Christmas. This activity gives the whole story from her point of view and uses lines from her famous "Magnificat" prayer (Luke 1:46–55) like a refrain. The activity is long but designed so it can be shortened, using the first six lines and the last six lines to frame almost any section the teacher wants to use. (To tell the Christmas story, for instance, stop just before the wedding at Cana and then skip to the final six lines.) Use "Mary's Story" also in May, which is Mary's month, or in October, when you teach the mysteries of the rosary, or to celebrate her birthday on September 8th. Mary's story embraces the entire liturgical year, because her story is also Jesus' story, and our story too.

When the angel first came to me,
(flap arms as angel's wings)

I was afraid.
(cower)

I didn't understand what was happening.
(tap forehead with forefinger, look puzzled)

But I didn't need to understand right away.
(shrug shoulders)

God had done great things for me,
(point to self in amazement)

and holy is God's name.
(raise hands high in praise)

I hurried to see my cousin Elizabeth.
(run in place)

She was going to have a baby too!
(pat tummy)

Her husband Zachary couldn't believe it,
(shake head "no")

so he had to stay mute.
(clasp hands over mouth tightly)

He couldn't talk till his baby was born.
(rock "baby" in arms)

Then he said, "His name will be John!"
(continue to rock baby, but display it proudly)

He agreed with me:
(point to self)

God had done great things for him,
(point to "him" offstage, amazed)

and holy is God's name.
(raise hands high in praise)

You all know about MY baby's birth...
(pat tummy)

What a time that was!
(shake head in wonderment)

Angels singing "Glory in the highest..."
(flap arms)

Wise men riding camels...
(hold "reins" and bounce as if riding)

Shepherds coming from all around...
(sweep arms widely on "all around")

Joseph having a dream to warn us...
(pillow hands under head)

Escaping to Egypt in the nick of time!
(gallop hurriedly in place)

One thing was certainly true:
(hold up one finger)

God had done great things for me,
(point to self, amazed)

and holy is God's name.
(raise hands high in praise)

Things settled down after a while.
(with palms down, lower hands in stages)

We moved back to Nazareth,
(slow, riding motions, plodding on a "donkey")

where Jesus did his chores every day.
(sweeping motions, then pick up items from floor)

He was growing up fast.
(measure with hand, indicating taller and taller)

When he was twelve we went to Jerusalem.
(walk vigorously in place, holding "pack" over shoulder)

Jesus liked listening to the teachers in the Temple.
(cup ear, nodding, thoughtful)

On the way home, I thought he was with Joseph's group.
(point offstage)

But Joseph thought he was with me!
(point to self, shaking head)

Jesus was lost back in the city!
(point "back there" behind you)

How worried we were!
(hold sides of head in hands and fret)

We rushed back to Jerusalem.
(run in place)

And there Jesus was,
(point in astonishment)

in the Temple, teaching!
(make "preaching" gestures)

We scolded him because we were worried.
(shake forefinger)

He said, "I must be about my father's business."
(point to heaven)

I didn't understand what he meant,
(shake head in wonderment)

but I trusted one thing:
(hold up one finger)

God had done great things for me,
(point to self, amazed)

and holy is God's name.
(raise hands high in praise)

One time we were at a wedding,
(raise glass as in a toast)

and they ran out of wine.
(drink out of "empty" glass, then turn it upside down and shake it)

I knew in my heart Jesus could help them.
(place hand over heart)

"Do whatever he tells you," I told the servants.
(give orders, pointing with finger)

Jesus said, "My hour has not yet come,"
(shake head "no")

but then he told them to bring six water jars.
(count out six jars in a row, one by one)

He prayed and the water turned to wine!
(bow head, fold hands in deep prayer)

One thing burned deep in my heart.
(hold up one finger)

God had done great things for me,
(point to self, amazed)

and holy is God's name.
(raise hands high in praise)

Jesus began to heal blind people.
(cover eyes, then remove hands, blinking)

And to heal deaf people.
(cover ears, then cup hands behind them, alert)

And he preached and told stories.
(make preaching gestures with hands)

Crowds came from all over to hear him.
(make wide sweeping motions with hands)

Jesus' enemies soon became jealous.
(scowl, hunch shoulders, grow furtive)

I didn't understand it.
(shake head, puzzled)

But I did trust one thing.
(hold up one finger)

God had done great things for me,
(point to self, amazed)

and holy is God's name.
(raise hands high in praise)

You all know what happened after that...
(point to everyone on "all")

How they arrested Jesus and took him to Pilate...
(walk in place with hands "tied" behind back, head bowed)

How the soldiers spit on him and whipped him...
(make whipping motions)

How they crowned him with thorns...
(wince as you press "crown" down on your head)

And hammered nails in his hands and feet...
(point to palms of hands and to feet)

And then crucified him.
(spread out arms as if nailed to cross, bow head)

I almost couldn't stand to watch.
(shield eyes, droop shoulders)

I almost couldn't trust the one thing I knew.
(hold up one finger)

God had *asked* great things of me,
(point to self, sorrowful)

and holy is God's name.
(raise hands high in praise)

But then came the Resurrection.
(make "raising up" motions with arms)

We were all so surprised!
(clap hands on both cheeks)

What did it all mean?
(shrug questioningly)

Jesus stayed for forty days trying to explain.
(make talking and "explaining" gestures)

Then he ascended back to heaven.
(point and look upward slowly as if watching it)

And on Pentecost the Holy Spirit came.
(cup hands in shape of flame over your head)

We all felt so strong!
(flex muscles)

The disciples started preaching everywhere.
(make wide, sweeping motions for "everywhere")

They baptized people by the hundreds.
(pour water over imaginary heads)

They had courage even when they were afraid.
(flex muscles)

They were all able to say one thing with me:
(hold up one finger)

God has done great things for me,
(point to self, amazed)

and holy is God's name.
(raise arms high in praise)

You too are able to say:
(point to group, individually)

God has done great things for me,
(point to self, amazed)

and holy is God's name.
(raise arms high in praise)

We are ALL able to say:
(sweep arms wide, inclusively)

God has done great things for me,
(point to self, amazed)

and HOLY IS GOD'S NAME!
(raise arms high in praise)

Questions for Discussion

Consider saying the "Hail Mary" with the children to prepare them for the discussion:

• Did Mary and Joseph understand everything that happened to Jesus?

• What gives *you* courage and strength when you don't understand what's happening?

• Can you think of one thing about Mary that is a little bit like you?

• Should everybody be able to say, "God has done great things for me"? What keeps us from doing so?

• Name two "great things" God has done for you.

Closing Prayer

Thank you, Lord, for giving us your Blessed Mother to be our mother too. Let us learn from her humility and obedience. Let us learn from her sense of wonder and from her eagerness to help others. Keep us faithful to you when we don't understand what's happening around us. Help us to trust the surprising ways you work "great things" in all our lives. Amen.

Nothing Could Stop St. Paul

Almost from the day of his death, St. Paul has been called simply "The Apostle," though he was not one of the original twelve. His vision on the Damascus road was so powerful it changed his life and shaped the whole Christian experience. It's described in three different places in the Scriptures, and the church celebrates it with a feast day all its own: The Conversion of St. Paul on January 25th. Paul's letters are the earliest written accounts of the gospel message, but he had no idea when he wrote them that they would one day be considered "Scripture" and part of the "New Testament." As a follow-up to this echo pantomime, invite older students to read one of Paul's shorter letters to see how his fiery personality jumps off the page.

One day Saul was riding to Damascus.
(gallop in place with a determined expression)

He was not named St. Paul yet.
(shake head)

Saul was mad and *nothing* could stop him.
(shake head and sweep hands in a horizontal "X": nothing)

He was *mad* at those new Christians.
(scowl and shake fist in the air)

He had a paper in his hot little hand...
(wave imaginary "paper" to show authority)

that would throw all Christians in jail.
(sweep hand horizontally, throwing them away)

He galloped faster and faster.
(gallop faster, more furiously)

Suddenly his horse stopped.
(make noise of screeching brakes, jerk to a stop)

Paul fell off his high horse.
(fall to the ground)

A bright light was shining all around.
(spread fingers wide, trace a large circle in front of face)

Paul was blinded and couldn't see a thing,
(cover eyes, flinch)

but he heard a loud voice.
(cup hand behind ear on "heard")

"Saul, Saul, why are you persecuting me?"
(speak through "megaphone" with hands around mouth)

"Who are you, Lord?" he said.
(shrug shoulders, spread hands outward, face upward)

"I am Jesus, and you are persecuting me."
(speak through "megaphone")

Paul was blinded for three days.
(hold up three fingers)

His friends took him home by the hand.
(hold an imaginary hand, take a few stumbling steps, eyes closed)

Then God sent a Christian to heal him.
(put hands over eyes, uncover suddenly, and blink)

Paul went out to the desert for a few years
(gallop in place)

to think and to pray.
(tap temple on "think" and fold hands on "pray")

He made tents out of goatskins.
(sewing motions)

He thought,
(fold fist under chin: "The Thinker")

and he prayed.
(fold hands in prayer)

Then he started preaching about Jesus.
(fling one arm out, mouthing words as an "orator")

His enemies wanted to kill him.
(slit throat, bare teeth)

His friends sneaked him out of the city at night.
(tiptoe in place, finger to lips: "sshhh")

They lowered him in a basket over the city wall.
(turn to the side, lean over, pull on "rope" as if lowering)

Nothing **could stop St. Paul.**
(shake head, sweep hands in horizontal "X": nothing)

When people in one place got mad at him,
(shake fist, bare teeth, snarl)

he would shake the dust off his feet
(shake dust off feet)

and go someplace else to preach about Jesus.
(turn to side and walk in place)

One time people stoned him.
(pick up "stones" and throw, angrily)

They left him for dead.
(droop head, close eyes)

But he got up and brushed himself off.
(brush yourself off)

Nothing could stop St. Paul.
(shake head, sweep hands in horizontal "X": nothing)

Another time Paul had a dream.
(pillow head on hands, close eyes in sleep)

"Come over and preach in Europe," he dreamt.
(motion "come here, come here")

So he traveled and preached some more.
(preached, "orator" motions)

Once they threw him in jail,
(fall to floor as if thrown, hold hand up to fend off attack)

and chained up his feet.
(stick feet up together as if chained)

But Paul and his friend sang God's praise,
(singing motions as if in an opera)

and suddenly there was an earthquake,
(remain on floor, shake and tilt and roll)

and their chains fell off.
(stand up, shaking each foot free, awestruck)

Nothing could stop St. Paul.
(shake head, sweep hands in horizontal "X": nothing)

He preached and preached about Jesus.
(preaching, "orator" motions)

And he healed so many people who were sick
(bend over, limp, then stand erect, walk proudly)

that they would take Paul's handkerchiefs
(slap back pocket and come up empty, mystified)

and use them to heal other people.
(dab arms of those nearby)

One time Paul preached so long
(preaching, "orator" motions)

that it got to be past midnight.
(tap "watch" on wrist)

A boy sitting in a window sill fell asleep,
(close eyes and nod head as if falling asleep)

and fell out the window.
(make an arc with hands describing the fall down, down)

He fell three floors down and died.
(hold up three fingers, close eyes and drop head)

Paul ran down and picked him up.
(run, then stoop to pick up imaginary "youth")

The boy came back to life.
(rub eyes, stretch, and yawn)

Nothing could stop St. Paul.
(shake head, sweep hands horizontally in an "X": nothing)

Five times he was whipped almost to death.
(whipping motions)

But he kept traveling and preaching about Jesus.
(gallop on horse, then stop and "preach")

And he kept writing letters.
(writing motions)

Three times he was beaten with clubs.
(clubbing, thrashing motions)

But he kept traveling and preaching about Jesus.
(gallop on horse, then stop and "preach")

And writing *more* letters.
(faster and faster writing motions)

Three times he was shipwrecked.
(hold up three fingers)

But *still* he kept traveling and preaching.
(gallop and "preach")

And writing *more* and *more* and MORE letters.
(even faster writing motions, wipe sweat from brow)

***Nothing* could stop St. Paul.**
(shake head, sweep hands in a horizontal "X": nothing)

Finally Roman soldiers tried to whip him,
(begin whipping motions, but halt)

but Paul said, "I appeal to Caesar!"
(arm extended, rigid, as in "Hail Caesar")

"I'm a Roman citizen, I must be taken to Rome."
(point to self, tap chest)

In Rome he spent two years under arrest.
(hold up two fingers)

People came to his house to hear him preach.
(walk in place, hurrying, cup ear to hear)

And Paul wrote even *MORE*—
(questioning tone, wait for children to holler "LETTERS," then nod and make writing motions)

***NOTHING* could stop St. Paul.**
(shake head, sweep hands in horizontal "X": nothing)

Finally the Romans chopped off his head.
(bend head down, make chopping motion at back of neck)

But even *this* didn't stop St. Paul!
(shake head, make sweeping "X" in amazement)

His friends kept reading his letters.
(hold up "scroll," move head side to side, reading)

People made copies for their friends.
(writing motions)

They gathered them all together.
(pick up imaginary letters and put them in a sheaf)

Paul's letters were the earliest part of the New Testament.
(open book as if reading Bible)

Even after he was dead, people could hear him preaching!
(preaching, "orator" motions)

***Nothing* could stop St. Paul.**
(shake head, make X with hands: "nothing")

Nothing could separate him from the love of Christ.
(point to heaven)

Nothing! Nothing! Nothing!
(repeat "nothing" motions decisively)

And nothing can separate *us* from the love of Christ!
(point to heaven)

Nothing! Nothing! Nothing!
(repeat "nothing" motions with finality)

Questions for Discussion

When the children are seated, hold up a copy of the New Testament and show them just how many epistles are Paul's. Then begin discussion:

- Do you like to write letters? Do you save really good letters that people write you?

- Paul earned his living by working as a tentmaker. What kind of work do you want to do when you grow up?

- Are most people afraid to speak out because of what others might think of them? Was Paul?

- Do you know anyone who has spoken out courageously even when it was unpopular?

- What kind of person would keep coming back after being shipwrecked and whipped and stoned and imprisoned?

Closing Prayer

Lord Jesus, you revealed yourself to Paul and changed his life. Help us also to see you on the road we're traveling, and let us change our lives however they need changing. Give us the courage to follow you even when it's not popular. Keep reminding us that nothing can ever separate us from your love. Raise up more leaders to serve you with energy like St. Paul's. Amen.

Who Was
St. Valentine,
Anyway?

St. Valentine was a priest and physician in Rome, martyred in the year 269 under the Emperor Claudius II. Little else is reliably known about him. The legends given here are delightful, but still only legends, though it's entirely possible our priest-physician-martyr healed the eyesight of the jailer's daughter and left her a farewell note, the first "Valentine." Some scholars think Valentine's famous patronage of sweethearts is a survival of the pagan Lupercalia festival which occurred on his feast day, and occasionally church leaders have tried to infuse more Christianity into the popular celebrations. St. Francis de Sales made young people choose saints' names and imitate their good works for the following year, but substituting saints for sweethearts didn't catch on in his time any more than it would in our own.

On Valentine's Day we all run around
(run in place)

cutting out red paper hearts,
(mime cutting out a heart)

giving people chocolates,
(pretend to hand out candy)

and sweet-smelling flowers.
(mime holding flower up to nose, sniff)

But why do we do all this?
(shrug, turn palms up, questioning)

Who was St. Valentine anyway?
(scratch head, puzzled)

Telling people we love them
(hands over heart)

is always a good idea...
(tap head, nod)

But what does St. Valentine have to do with it?
(scratch head, puzzled)

It's a long story.
(twirl forefinger, spinning out a story)

St. Valentine lived in Rome a long time ago,
(jerk thumb serval times over shoulder: "ago")

about 200 years after Jesus.
(hold up two fingers for two hundred)

The emperor in those days was a tough old soldier,
(stand at attention, salute)

who wanted more soldiers to ride off to war.
(gallop in place)

And he had the idea
(tap forehead)

that if soldiers were *married*,
(mime putting wedding ring on finger)

they wouldn't want to ride off to war...
(gallop in place, shaking head)

They'd want to stay *home*...
(point to ground: "stay here")

So the emperor outlawed marriage.
(hold up hands: "Whoa!" "Stop!")

He said *nobody* could get engaged or married.
(shake head arrogantly, fold arms across chest)

Valentine was a priest who heard about this,
(cup ear to hear)

and decided to marry young couples in secret.
(put finger to lips as in "shh, shh," look around secretively)

Many young people came to him,
(tiptoe in place, stealthily)

and got married secretly.
(mime putting ring on finger, look over shoulder as if worried)

The young couples were happy about this.
(turn up corners of mouth with fingers)

They loved the priest who helped them.
(hands over heart)

For a long time things were okay.
(tap wristwatch)

But finally Valentine was betrayed
(whisper behind hand, point offstage with other hand)

for breaking the Emperor's law.
(mime snapping an imaginary stick in half)

He was marched off to jail,
(march, hands behind back as if handcuffed, bow head)

and condemned to death.
(slit throat with finger)

But Valentine wasn't sad in prison.
(pull edges of mouth down, shake head)

He stayed cheerful,
(turn up mouth with fingers)

because the young people wrote him letters of love,
(writing motions)

and threw flowers in his window.
(toss "flowers" as if basketball)

Was that the beginning of Valentines?
(shrug shoulders, palms out, questioning look)

Nobody knows for sure.
(shake head)

But it's good to remember
(tap forehead)

that Valentine had so much love,
(hands over heart)

he laid down his life for his friends.
(shut eyes, droop head)

And it's always a good idea
(tap head, nod)

to tell people we love them.
(hands over heart)

Now, the jailer had a daughter who was blind.
(cover eyes with hands)

She brought Valentine food to eat,
(eating motions)

and he healed her blindness.
(close eyes, then pry them open with fingers, blink)

Suddenly she could see everything!
(shade eyes and look around, blinking)

Valentine wrote the little girl a note
(writing motions)

the night before he was killed,
(slit throat with finger)

and signed it: "From Your Valentine."
(make signature with a flourish)

And she could read it with her own eyes!
(point to eyes, amazed)

Was that the beginning of Valentines?
(shrug shoulders, palms out, questioning look)

Nobody knows for sure.
(shake head)

But it's always a good idea
(tap head, nod)

to tell people we love them.
(hands over heart)

The day that Valentine got killed
(slit throat with finger)

was a carnival time of games and dancing.
(pretend to dance with partner)

When young men would draw names
(cover eyes with one hand, draw name from "box" with other)

to see who their partners would be.
(shade eyes, look around to see)

Later on when the Romans became Christian,
(mark cross on forehead with thumb)

they kept the parties and dancing,
(dance in place with "partner")

and honored Valentine, the patron of sweethearts.
(pucker up, make smooching noises)

Was that the beginning of Valentines?
(shrug shoulders, palms out, questioning)

Nobody knows for sure.
(shake head)

But it's always a good idea
(tap head, nod)

to tell people we love them.
(hands over heart)

Not just sweethearts,
(pucker up, make smooching noises)

but friends and family too.
(point around room)

It's always a good idea
(tap head, nod)

to tell people we love them.
(hands over heart)

Questions for Discussion

After the children sit down, prompt their discussion with questions like these:

- Do you know how to cut out a heart from construction paper? Do you like making Valentines?

- What other ways do you show that you love people, not just on Valentine's Day?

- Is anyone you know a shut-in? What kind of Valentine will you send them?

- Is it hard or easy to tell people you like them (or love them)? Is it embarrassing to hear people tell you the same thing?

- Are you sending Valentines just to your special friends this year? Can you think of someone who would be surprised to get one from you?

Closing Prayer

Father, as we celebrate St. Valentine's Day, we thank you for giving us the gift of love and friendship. We ask that others "know we are Christians by our love," especially the love we show to those who need it most. Give us courage to reach out to others who are different from ourselves, and let us rejoice that your loving kindness touches us all. Amen.

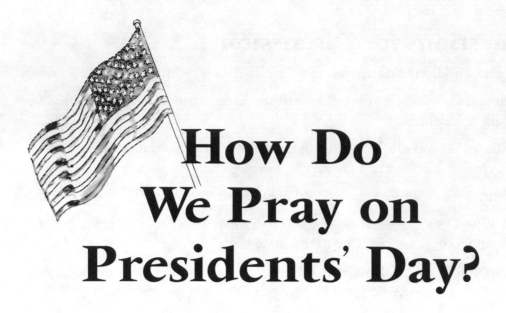

How Do We Pray on Presidents' Day?

Presidents Day, the third Monday in February, honors two of our greatest Presidents—George Washington and Abraham Lincoln— who both had birthdays in February. The holiday gives us a chance to talk about honesty, leadership, and service to our country. It's also an opportunity to remind our students that we have an obligation to offer "supplications, prayers, intercessions, and thanksgivings" for all those in high positions, "so that we may lead a quiet and peaceable life in all godliness and dignity" (1 Timothy 2:2). Most of us remember to pray for the pope, but few people remember to pray for the president. Maybe it's time we should!

George Washington was a tall, tall man.
(reach high to indicate height)

He was our very first president.
(hold up one finger)

One of the best presidents we've ever had!
(make circle with thumb and forefinger: "the best")

He rode his horse all over his plantation
(turn to right, gallop in place)

and all around the wilderness as a surveyor.
(turn to left, gallop in place)

Then he became a general for the colonists.
(salute snappily)

And after that the first president.
(salute even more snappily)

There's a story about him as a little boy
(indicate "so tall")

that he never told a lie.
(clamp both hands across mouth, shake head)

Once when he got a new little hatchet,
(two-handed chopping motions)

he practiced chopping sticks and branches.
("chop" in three distinct places around you)

And then he looked for something bigger.
(peer around, shading eyes)

He saw a cherry tree, just the right size.
(point "offstage," excitedly)

And cheerfully he chopped it down!
(chop away with a big smile)

But when his father came home,
(turn to side, stomp sternly in place)

he said, "Who chopped down my cherry tree?"
(deep voice, point accusingly at several children)

George Washington spoke right up.
(wave right hand in air to get attention)

"I cannot tell a lie, Father,"
(shake head)

"I was the one."
(point to self with both hands)

"I chopped it down with my new little hatchet."
(chopping motions)

George thought his father would get mad.
(make "mad" face)

But he didn't.
(shake head, amazed)

He was happy that George didn't tell a lie.
(turn up edges of mouth with forefingers)

Everyone respected George Washington.
(sweep arms widely on "everyone")

They threw flowers at him when he was elected President.
(mime pelting someone with flowers)

They said he was "First in war,"
(hold up one finger on right hand)

"first in peace,"
(hold up one finger on left hand)

"and first in the hearts of his countrymen."
(hold hands over heart)

We thank *God* for George Washington.
(point to heaven)

We pray for more leaders like him.
(hands folded in prayer)

Abraham Lincoln was also a tall, tall man.
(reach high to indicate height)

And he wore a tall stovepipe hat.
(pat head, then measure "tall hat," stretching high)

Everybody called him "Honest Abe."
(wave hand as if in greeting)

When he was a little boy,
(indicate "so big")

his pioneer family was poor,
(turn imaginary pockets inside out, empty)

and he wasn't able to go to school.
(shake head)

But he loved to read books.
(open palms together like a book)

He used to stay up late,
(tap wristwatch)

reading by the light of the log fire.
(open palms like book, reading hungrily)

He studied hard to become a lawyer.
(read intently, moving head back and forth)

And traveled from town to town
(turn to right, gallop in place)

as a circuit riding lawyer.
(turn to left, gallop faster in place)

Abraham Lincoln did *not* like slavery.
(shake head firmly)

He gave speeches about it,
(make "orator" motions, sweeping arm outward)

and wrote letters about it,
(writing motions)

and gave more speeches.
("orator" motions)

Half the states did *not* want slavery.
(shake head)

But half the states *did*.
(nod head, make "rah, rah" motions)

It was not an easy time to be president.
(shake head sadly)

The North and the South were fighting.
(spar with fists)

It made President Lincoln sad.
(turn down corners of mouth, "sad face")

But Abraham Lincoln had courage.
(flex muscles, stand up straight)

He signed the Emancipation Proclamation.
(sign, with a flourish)

And freed *all* the slaves.
(sweep arms widely on "all")

The war lasted for four long years.
(hold up four fingers)

It made Lincoln's heart heavy.
(hands over heart, droop body slightly)

But finally the war ended.
(hold up hands as in "Whoa, stop")

All the soldiers marched back home.
(turn to side, march in place)

Lincoln had kept the country together.
(grip both hands together)

Lincoln had ended slavery.
(hold up hands as in "Whoa, stop")

We thank *God* for Abraham Lincoln.
(point to heaven)

We pray for more leaders like him.
(hands folded in prayer)

How do we pray on Presidents Day?
(shrug shoulders, turn hands up, questioning)

First we pray thank you to God
(hold up one finger, then point to heaven)

for those two famous presidents.
(hold up two fingers)

Then we pray for future leaders, like you...
(point around to individual people)

and you, and you.
(keep pointing)

And we pray for all who lead us *today*.
(point to ground, "here and now")

We pray for them to be wise,
(tap temple with forefinger)

and to have good hearts,
(hands over heart)

and to be obedient to God.
(point to heaven)

That's how we pray on Presidents Day.
(hands folded in prayer)

Not just for Abe and George,
(shake head)

but for all our leaders, all the time.
(sweep arms widely)

That's how we pray on Presidents Day.
(hands folded in prayer, nod head)

That's how we pray on Presidents Day.
(hands folded in prayer, nod head)

Questions for Discussion

Let the children sit down and then ask them these questions:

- Whose picture is on one dollar bills? On five dollar bills? On pennies? On quarters?

- How would you feel if *you* were caught chopping down a cherry tree?

- Is it sometimes hard not to lie?

- Who is president now? How can we remember to pray for him?

- What other government positions do you know about? (governor, mayor, vice president, judges, etc.) Shall we find out their names and begin praying for them too?

Closing Prayer

Heavenly Father, thank you for giving us courageous presidents like George Washington and Abraham Lincoln. Please raise up more good leaders for our country and help them make wise decisions for our future. Amen.

Ashes, Ashes, We All Fall Down

Ash Wednesday begins the church's forty-day period of preparation for Easter. The three traditional practices of Lent—fasting, alms-giving and prayer—have not gone out of style since Vatican II, as many people think. However, these disciplines cannot become ends in themselves, but must be a means of conversion and returning to our baptismal promises—a tall order for teachers and parents! For the idea of "conversion," our echo pantomime uses the notion of "getting priorities straight," and we don't hedge on the word "sacrifice." Since Old Testament times, "strewing dust on their heads and rolling in ashes" (Ezekiel 27:30) has been a symbol of repentance, which is why we receive ashes at the start of this penitential season. Older students will like hearing that the ashes they receive this year are made by burning last year's palms from Palm Sunday.

Do you remember the nursery rhyme
(tap forehead)

"Ashes, Ashes, We All Fall Down?"
(fall dramatically to the ground)

Well, when we fall down,
(speak from on the ground, pat the floor)

we have to pick ourselves up again
(get up, stretch legs, shake them)

and dust ourselves off.
(brush dust off clothes)

And that's what Lent is like.
(straighten and shake legs again, dust self off)

We need to prepare ourselves for Easter.
(extend arms as in Crucifixion, then raise arms to "Risen")

We get ashes on Ash Wednesday
(mark cross on forehead with thumb)

to remind us
(snap fingers, hold up forefinger: "That's it!")

that we come from ashes and dust,
(point offstage in one direction)

and we'll wind up ashes and dust.
(point offstage in other direction)

Remember in the book of Genesis,
(open hands as if reading book)

how God formed Adam from the dust of the earth
(stoop to pick up "earth," pretend to model clay)

and breathed his Spirit into him?
(cup hands around mouth and blow gently)

That reminds us who we are,
(point to everybody)

and how to get our priorities straight.
(use hand to indicate a "list" in the air, top to bottom)

God comes first.
(hold up one finger, extend arm high)

Everything else winds up dust and ashes.
(dust yourself off)

Jesus went off to the desert
(turn to side, walk in place)

to fast and pray for forty days.
(bow head, fold hands in prayer)

In Lent we follow his footsteps.
(turn to side, walk in place)

And try to get our priorities straight.
(use hand to indicate a "list" in the air, top to bottom)

God comes *first!*
(hold up one finger, extend arm high)

So we pray
(bow head, fold hands in prayer)

and make sacrifices to *remember* this.
(tap forehead)

Everybody makes sacrifices
(point around room to "everybody")

when they want one thing more than another.
(hold out hands as a "balance scale," weighing one hand higher)

Sometimes we sacrifice a little sleep,
(pillow head in hands)

in order to start a trip early in the morning.
(yawn, rub eyes, stretch)

Sometimes we sacrifice lots of energy,
(look exhausted, pant, wipe brow)

in order to work out and get in shape.
(do jumping jacks)

Lent asks everybody to sacrifice,
(sweep arm to indicate "everybody")

in order to grow closer to God.
(point to heavens)

Maybe by eating a "Rice Bowl" meal,
(make tiny eating motions)

instead of a big fancy meal,
(make big eating motions, two-fisted, gobble)

to give us hearts concerned for the poor,
(put hands over heart)

and to give them the extra money.
(reach in pocket, give away "money")

Lent asks everybody
(sweep arm to indicate "all")

to spend extra time praying,
(bow head, fold hands in prayer)

or reading the Bible,
(open hands as if reading a book)

or going to daily Mass if we can,
(turn to side and walk in place)

so we can grow closer to God.
(point to heavens)

Where does this extra time come from?
(shrug shoulders, hands outward)

Maybe from sacrificing a little play time.
(pretend to jump hopscotch, then stop abruptly)

Maybe from turning off the TV.
(reach over, turn off "knob")

We sacrifice one thing that's good
(hold up one finger)

for something that's better,
(point to heavens)

in order to get our priorities straight.
(use hand to indicate a "list" in the air, top to bottom)

God comes *first!*
(hold up one finger, extend arm high)

Everything else winds up dust and ashes.
(dust self off)

People who are old enough,
(make "so high" measurements)

use Lent as a special time
(point to wristwatch)

to go to confession,
(bow head, cross self)

because like the nursery rhyme says,
(make "talking" motions)

"We all fall down,"
(fall dramatically to ground)

and need to pick ourselves up again,
(get up, stretch out legs and shake them)

and dust ourselves off.
(brush dust off clothes)

And confession helps us "dust ourselves off."
(make sign of cross)

I love getting ashes on Ash Wednesday.
(mark cross on forehead with thumb)

I don't mind wearing them all day.
(shake head)

I don't mind people asking what they mean.
(point, raise eyebrows questioningly)

It makes me want with all my heart
(cover heart with hands)

to get my priorities straight.
(Use hand to indicate a "list" in the air, top to bottom)

To remember above all things
(tap forehead firmly)

God is *first!*
(hold up one finger, extend arm high)

And that's the best priority of all!
(raise hands in praise)

God is *first!*
(hold up one finger, extend arm high)

And that's the best priority of all!
(raise hands in praise)

Questions for Discussion

Start your discussion of Ash Wednesday and Lent with these questions:

• On Ash Wednesday, will you leave the ashes on your forehead all day?

• What will you say if people ask you about your ashes?

• What new habits of praying do you want to form this Lent?

• Do you know anyone who uses the "Rice Bowl" during Lent? How will you gather "sacrifice" money as a parish?

- Can you remember a time you "sacrificed" one good thing in order to have something you wanted more?

Closing Prayer

Heavenly Father, help us discipline ourselves this Lent so that your will is our top priority. Show us new habits you want us to form, and old habits you'd like us to break. Bring us always closer to the footsteps of Jesus, Our Savior. Really renew us so we'll be ready to celebrate Easter this year with a new joy. Amen.

Moses and the People Who Grumbled

Moses and the Israelites spent forty years in the desert before reaching the Promised Land. We spend forty days of Lent reflecting on many of the same lessons of that desert experience. Grumbling is not seen as a sin these days (in fact it's become a national pastime), but your students will think twice about it after this echo story. Learning to say thank you to God is never out of season. But since we combine the theme of manna in the wilderness with the eucharist, this activity is especially suited for use during Lent or for first communion preparation. As a follow-up to the story, challenge your older students to see how closely this version follows the Scriptures: (Exodus 16:1–36; 17:1–7; Numbers 11:4–15; John 6:48–51). The amusing idea of "manna pancakes" is found in the Jerusalem Bible's translation of Numbers 11:8.

After Moses and his people ran away from mean old Pharaoh,
(run in place)

and after all the mean old Pharaoh's soldiers drowned in the Red Sea,
(hold nose with one hand, raise other for help, sink down in place saying, "blub, blub, blub")

they had a long, hot walk across the desert.
(walk in place, wiping off sweat)

A *forty-year* long, hot walk across the desert!
(walk slower and slower, slump)

The people began to *grumble* against Moses.
(screw up face, mumble "grumble, grumble" under breath)

And they *complained* against Moses.
(make "complain-complain-complain" noises)

And they *murmured* against Moses.
(mumble "murmur-murmur-murmur")

They were a people who *forgot* to say "Thank you!"
(slap forehead on "forgot")

They didn't know yet that "Eucharist" *means* "Thank you."
(spread hands wide, heavenward)

"MO-SES!" the people whined.
(hold nose to make "MO-SES!" sound whiny)

"We're thirsty!"
(point to open mouth, roll eyes upward)

"There's no water out here in this desert!"
(shake head for "no water")

"We're so thirsty we're gonna *die!*"
(clasp throat as if dying of thirst)

"We wanna go back to Egypt!"
(turn around abruptly 180 degrees, then run in place)

So Moses patiently prayed to God,
(fold hands in prayer)

and God patiently heard his prayer.
(cup ear on "heard")

He told Moses to take up his staff,
(hold up imaginary "staff")

And strike a rock with it.
(hit imaginary "rock," making a "whap, whap" sound)

Water gushed forth from the rock.
(with hands, make an arc in the air on "gushed")

The people drank their fill.
(cup hands to scoop water, make "slurp, slurp" sounds)

But they *forgot* to say "Thank you."
(slap forehead on "forgot")

They didn't know yet that "Eucharist" *means* "Thank you."
(spread hands wide, heavenward)

So the people grumbled against Moses again.
(lower head, scowl, make "grumble, grumble" sounds)

And they murmured again.
(keep scowling, say "murmur, murmur" under breath)

"MO-SES!" the people whined.
(hold nose to sound whiny)

"We're hungry!"
(rub tummy)

"There's no *food* out here in this desert."
(shake head on "no")

"We're so hungry, we're gonna *die!*"
(clasp throat as if dying)

"We wanna go back to Egypt!"
(turn around abruptly 180 degrees, run in place)

So Moses prayed patiently to God *again*.
(fold hands in prayer)

And *again* God heard his prayer.
(cup ear on "heard")

God sent *manna* from heaven.
(imitate falling rain, with fingers fluttering down)

Every morning manna was on the ground like dew.
(point all around on ground, excitedly)

It was white and powdery and sweet to the taste.
(lick lips as in "yum, yum")

And it made terrific pancakes!
(flip pancakes)

The people ate their fill.
(eat two-fistedly, make "gobble, gobble" sounds)

But they *forgot* to say "Thank you."
(slap forehead on "forgot")

They didn't know yet that "Eucharist" means "Thank you."
(spread hands wide and look heavenward)

God said *not* to gather more than they needed.
(shake finger on "not")

And *not* to hoard it away.
(shake finger again, warning)

But some of the people were *greedy*.
(make "gimme, gimme" motions)

And some of them were *lazy*.
(yawn, stretch, look bored)

And they tried to do it anyway.
(hunch over and make "sneaky" motions of hiding, hoarding)

The next day their manna was all rotten and smelly.
(hold nose as in "phew!")

So *again* the people grumbled against Moses.
(scowl, pout, make "grumble, grumble" sounds)

And *again* they murmured.
(make "murmur-murmur" sounds)

"MO-SES!" the people whined.
(hold nose to draw out whiny sounds)

"We're *tired* of all this manna!"
(push manna away, fold arms and pout)

"Manna, manna, manna, same old thing every day!"
(scowl, fold arms, pout)

"We want *meat!*"
(rub tummy)

"We want *cucumbers!*"
(rub tummy, lick lips, make smacking sounds)

"We want *melons!*"
(rub tummy, smack lips, rub hands together in anticipation)

"We wanna go back to Egypt!"
(turn around abruptly 180 degrees, run in place)

Moses was getting tired of these people.
(slump shoulders, droop head)

But he prayed anyway that God send them meat.
(fold hands in prayer)

And once again God heard his prayer.
(cup hand behind ear on "heard")

God sent *quails* flying in from the sea.
(flap arms like a bird)

Hundreds of quails.
(flap arms faster and faster)

Hundreds and hundreds and HUNDREDS of quails.
(flap arms faster, faster, faster, exhaustedly)

The people roasted the meat to eat.
(eating motions, make "gobble, gobble" sounds, lick lips)

They ate lots and *lots* of meat.
(faster and faster eating motions, lick lips faster)

But they *forgot* to say, "Thank you."
(slap forehead on "forgot")

They didn't know yet that "Eucharist" *means* "Thank you."
(spread hands wide, heavenward)

God kept his people in the desert a *long* time.
(tap wrist for wristwatch)

He *knew* they had to learn to say, "Thank you."
(tap forehead on "knew")

So Jesus came down to teach us
(point to self on "us")

that he is the Living Bread for the life of the *world*...
(spread arms wide on "world")

the bread that rains down like manna.
(make falling rain motions)

And that all who come to him won't ever be hungry,
(shake head, rub tummy)

And all who come to him won't ever be thirsty,
(point inside opened mouth, roll eyes upward)

And that "Eucharist" means "Thank you."
(spread arms wide, heavenward)

***We* don't want to be people who *forget* to say "Thank you."**
(slap forehead on "forget")

We *know* that "Eucharist" means "Thank you."
(spread arms wide, heavenward)

WE KNOW THAT "EUCHARIST" MEANS "THANK YOU!"
(louder, spread arms wide, heavenward)

WE KNOW THAT "EUCHARIST" MEANS...?
(much louder, inviting children to shout the words "thank you.")

Questions for Discussion

When the children shout back the answer to the final line of the echo story, the teacher should bow to them and applaud, and then have them sit down for questions:

- What things do kids your age usually grumble about?

- What should you do as soon as you realize you've been grumbling or complaining or whining?

- Do you say thank you to God after your meals? Do you say thank you to the person who cooks your meals?

- Count on your fingers at least five things to say thank you to God for today.

- How does holy communion remind us to say thank you to God?

Closing Prayer

Heavenly Father, too often we forget to say thank-you for all the things you give us each day. Too often we're like those people in the desert who grumbled and complained and whined. Too often we forget how wonderful the gift of Jesus in holy communion really is. Remind us frequently, O Lord, that "Eucharist means Thank you," and then keep expanding our grateful hearts until they are one with you. Amen.

St. Patrick Means More than Parades

March 17 is the feast of St. Patrick, "Apostle of Ireland" (about 387–461). The many legends, especially the one about lighting the great Easter fire at Tara, are true to the spirit of Patrick's accomplishments, even if we're not sure they're strictly historical. For thirty years he was almost as tireless in evangelizing as St. Paul himself. In Patrick's old age he wrote his "Confessions" (the word used for an autobiography) detailing his kidnapping and slavery. His little book—a scant sixty-two paragraphs—is humble and inspiring, full of the total trust in God that Patrick learned while enslaved by pagans. His prayer, St. Patrick's "Breastplate," which has several popular musical settings, would make a good accompaniment to celebrating his feast day.

Saint Patrick was a bishop.
(shape a bishop's hat over head)

On his feast day we march in parades,
(march, highstepping, pretend to blow trombone)

because he drove snakes out of Ireland,
(place forefingers side by side, move like wiggly snakes)

and used shamrocks to teach the Trinity.
(count off three fingers)

But Patrick wasn't even Irish.
(shake head, disbelieving)

And we don't know about the snakes.
(repeat wiggly fingers)

When Patrick was very young,
(hold hand horizontal to measure "so high")

he was kidnapped by pirates
(bow head, turn sideways, walk with hands "cuffed" behind back)

and taken to Ireland on a ship.
(draw "waves" in air with hand)

At this time the Irish weren't Christians.
(shake head sadly)

Patrick's head was shaved like all other slaves.
(rub top of head briskly)

His master made Patrick watch his pigs,
(shade eyes with hand, gaze around)

so Patrick had time to think about religion.
(adopt the "Thinker" pose)

And he gave his whole heart to God,
(hands over heart)

and spent much time in prayer.
(tap wristwatch)

He said at least a hundred prayers at night
(pillow head on hands as if sleeping)

and a hundred prayers by day.
(wake up, yawn, then quickly fold hands in prayer)

For six years he was a slave.
(hold up three fingers on each hand)

Then he had a dream.
(pillow head on hands)

A voice said, "Your ship is ready."
(make megaphone around mouth)

When Patrick woke up,
(yawn, stretch, rub eyes)

he ran two hundred miles to the coast
(run madly in place)

and boarded a ship and sailed away.
(draw "waves" in air with hand)

After three days it reached an unknown land.
(hold up three fingers)

For a whole month they walked around, lost.
(trudge, look around, and shrug)

Their food ran out.
(rub tummy, grimace)

The captain asked Patrick to pray,
(fold hands in prayer, bow head)

and a herd of wild pigs came running.
(run in place, little steps, snort)

They had *lots* of meat.
(rub tummy, smile, smack lips: "mmm")

When Patrick finally got home, his family was shocked...
(slap hands on both sides of face)

but happy to see how he'd grown.
(measure "so high" again, much taller)

Patrick studied for the priesthood.
(pretend to read a book)

And was made a bishop.
(shape a bishop's hat over head)

And then he had another dream.
(pillow head on hands)

He heard the voices of Ireland calling
(cup hand behind ear, listen)

"Come back, O holy youth!"
(beckon "come back")

So Patrick sailed back to Ireland again.
(draw "waves" in air with hand)

He told *everybody* about Jesus,
(spread arms wide for "everybody")

and founded churches and convents,
(make "rock" signs, one fist on other, as in "paper-scissors-rock")

and ordained priests.
(make cross on forehead with thumb)

Then one night during the Easter Vigil,
(hold up one finger)

he lit the Easter fire on a high hill,
(indicate "high hill")

which was seen all the way to Tara,
(shade eyes, peer into distance)

where the High King got angry!
(scowl, shake fist)

It was against the law to light the sacred fire!
(scowl, shake forefinger as in "no-no")

No one but the Druids could light it!
(shake head, act superior)

The Druids told the King an ancient prophecy:
(make "talking" gesture with thumb against forefingers)

unless the fire was put out that very night,
(wag forefinger, in warning)

it would *never* be extinguished in Ireland.
(shake head firmly on "never")

The King sent warriors against Patrick.
(point offstage commanding: "Go!")

They marched Patrick's men back, captive.
(turn to other side, march in place, hands behind back)

The Druids' servants were hiding and waiting.
(huddle down, secretively)

They wanted to kill the Christians marching by.
(still huddled, grin evilly, slit throat)

They heard them singing Patrick's prayer,
(cup hand behind ear, mystified)

but all they could see was a row of deer!
(counting, point to one-two-three..., squint)

Patrick told the High King about Jesus.
(stretch out arms as if crucified)

He said, "The Druids can bring darkness,"
(cover eyes for "darkness")

"But they can never bring light."
(shake head, firmly)

Then Patrick crisscrossed Ireland,
(make huge "X" in air with hand)

founding more churches, and convents, and schools.
(one fist on other, as in "paper-scissors-rock" game)

He wanted everybody to study and read.
(pore over imaginary book)

And he spoke against the practice of slavery.
(shake head, make "no-no" motion with hands)

The stories of Patrick go on and on and on.
(twirl one forefinger in a circle)

One day he went up a high mountain
(indicate "high" with one hand)

to bless the whole of Ireland before he died.
(make sign of cross north, east, south, west)

And God sent all the Irish saints to him,
(make "shoo, shoo" motions)

even the *future* saints, to join in the blessing,
(make sign of cross north, east, south, west)

so that before Patrick died,
(close eyes, droop head)

he could see *all* the saints whose father he was.
(shield eyes with hand, peer all around)

The Easter fire has never gone out in Ireland.
(shake head)

Pray that it never goes out in *you*...
(point to others for "you")

and never goes out in *me*.
(point to self, tap chest)

And meanwhile, LET'S JOIN THE PARADE!
(march highstepping, pretend to play trombone).

Questions for Discussion

Settle the group down and then talk about the following things:

- What comforts of home do you think Patrick missed when he was kidnapped?

- Have you seen the lighting of the Easter fire at the Easter Vigil Mass? What's it like to see the whole church go from darkness to light?

- How can you remember to pray when you're alone, away from family and friends?

- Patrick always regretted not being able to study when he was young—what subjects do you want to study harder?

- Does your parish songbook have St. Patrick's prayer of protection, called his "Breastplate"? Singing the beautiful words helps us remember it better.

Closing Prayer

O Most Holy Trinity, St. Patrick accepted with humility everything that happened to him. Whether slavery or success, he made the most of it and saw himself surrounded by your love, O Father, Son, and Holy Spirit. Give us a share in his courage, in his ability to work tirelessly, in his endurance of trouble, and above all give us his enthusiasm to spread your love to all those we meet. Amen.

St. Joseph
Was a Carpenter

St. Joseph is patron of the universal church, and also of workers, families, travelers, the poor, the sick, the dying, of those in authority, of priests and religious, of prayer and contemplation. His patronage is diverse because of the authority and practical responsibility he held in the Holy Family. In the Scriptures Joseph is a major character only in Matthew 1 and 2, the early life of Jesus. Because he's not mentioned afterwards, scholars assume he died before the time of Jesus' public ministry, and some writers have used this probability to speculate that Joseph was much older than Mary. Artists have frequently pictured Joseph as an old man, though there is no real evidence for it. St. Joseph has two feast days on the calendar: March 19, and also May 1, the feast of Joseph the Worker.

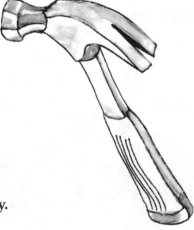

St. Joseph was a carpenter.
(make hammering motions)

He worked hard,
(hammer faster, in several places)

and prayed lots.
(fold hands, bow head)

He was engaged to a girl named Mary.
(point to ring finger, tapping)

And he was very, very happy.
(smile, fingers lifting corners of mouth)

One day Mary ran up to him.
(run in place)

She said, "An angel came to me!"
(flap arms like wings)

"I'm going to have a special, special baby!"
(pat tummy proudly)

Joseph didn't understand.
(shake head, frown, perplexed)

He was worried.
(frown, fold fist under chin like "The Thinker")

He thought he'd better not marry her.
(shake head, sadly)

Then he had a dream.
(pillow head on hands, sleeping)

An angel came to him
(flap arms like wings)

and said, "Don't be afraid."
(shake head)

"Go ahead and take Mary for your wife."
(point to ring finger, tapping)

"Name her baby, *JESUS*..."
(rock arms for baby)

"He will save his people from their sins."
(spread arms like crucifixion)

Joseph woke up.
(rub eyes, wonderingly)

He said "Yes" to all God had told him.
(nod head vigorously)

So Joseph and Mary got married.
(tap ring finger, proudly)

And Jesus was born at Bethlehem.
(rock "baby" in arms, proudly)

The Wise Men came with gifts.
(march, holding "gifts" in outstretched hands)

But King Herod was jealous.
(frown, stamp foot petulantly)

He hated this newborn king.
(frown, shake fist in air)

He planned to *kill* the Baby Jesus.
(slice finger across throat, grimacing)

He sent soldiers to kill all the baby boys.
(slice finger across throat repeatedly)

But Joseph had another dream.
(pillow head on hands, sleeping)

***Again* an angel came to him.**
(flap arms like wings)

"Run quickly with Jesus and Mary," the angel said.
(run in place)

"King Herod wants to kill Baby Jesus!"
(slice finger across throat)

"Run away to Egypt and stay there!"
(run in place)

Joseph woke up.
(rub eyes, wonderingly)

He said "Yes" to everything God had told him.
(Nod head vigorously)

He took Mary and Jesus and ran away to Egypt.
(run in place)

They lived there a long time.
(point to watch)

Then Joseph had *another* dream.
(pillow head on hands, sleeping)

Again an angel came to him.
(flap arms like wings)

"It's safe to go home now," the angel said.
(point offstage with thumb)

"Wicked King Herod has died."
(flop head on chest, eyes closed)

Joseph woke up.
(rub eyes, yawn, stretch)

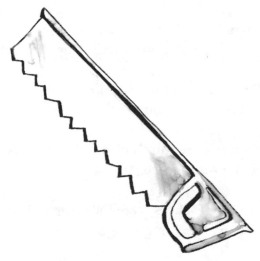

He said "Yes" to all God told him.
(nod vigorously)

They went back home to Nazareth.
(walk in place, happily)

They were happy to go home.
(turn up corners of mouth)

In Nazareth Jesus grew and grew.
(indicate increasing height, "so high")

Joseph taught him how to be a carpenter.
(hold up "nail," then show how to hammer it)

How to make tables and chairs out of wood.
(more hammering motions, and sawing)

Every year at Passover they walked to Jerusalem.
(walk in place)

When Jesus was twelve they went there as usual.
(indicate height of a twelve-year-old)

On the way home Joseph said, "Where's Jesus?"
(shrug, look around, puzzled)

Mary said, "I thought he was with *you*."
(point to "you")

"But I thought he was with *you!*" Joseph said.
(point in other direction)

"Oh, no! He's *lost!*" said Mary.
(put both hands to side of face in dismay)

They hurried back to Jerusalem to find him.
(run in place)

They looked and looked.
(look around, hand shading eyes)

For three days they looked.
(hold up three fingers)

Finally they found him in the Temple.
(point offstage excitedly)

All the teachers were listening to him.
(cup ear, nodding in agreement)

"We've been looking all over for you!" said Mary.
(look around, shading eyes)

"We were worried!"
(put both hands to side of face in dismay)

"Why were you looking for me?" Jesus said.
(shrug shoulders, turn up hands)

"Didn't you know I must be about my Father's business?"
(point upward to Father in heaven)

Joseph and Mary didn't understand.
(frown, shake head, perplexed)

But Jesus obeyed Joseph and Mary,
(salute snappily as in "Yes, sir!")

and went home to Nazareth with them.
(walk in place)

And he grew and grew and grew.
(indicate height, up, up, up to adult size)

After this the Bible doesn't mention Joseph any more.
(use hands as open book, shake head)

He wasn't there when Jesus started preaching.
(shake head sadly)

He must have died before that.
(drop head gently on chest, eyes closed)

But we love Joseph because Jesus loved him.
(hands over heart)

And because he took good care of Jesus and Mary.
(rock baby in arms, smile)

And because he worked hard.
(make hammering motions)

And listened to God in his dreams.
(pillow head on hands, sleeping)

And obeyed even when he didn't understand.
(shake head, perplexed)

Good St. Joseph, pray for us.
(make sign of cross and fold hands)

Holy St. Joseph, pray for us.
(make sign of cross and fold hands)

Amen. Amen.
(fold hands, nod twice)

Questions for Discussion

Tell the children to sit down, and use these questions to get them started:

- What sorts of things do you think St. Joseph taught Jesus when he was growing up?

- Have you ever made something with wood and hammer and nails?

- What would have happened to Jesus if St. Joseph hadn't obeyed *immediately* whenever he knew what God wanted him to do?

- Is it hard for most people to do things immediately? What makes us drag our feet?

- Do you know anyone who works hard but stays in the background? Are they a little bit like St. Joseph?

Closing Prayer

Good St. Joseph, God trusted you to be head of the Holy Family and you were faithful to your responsibility. Help us to live close to our Lord and to be good workers whether we're at home or away from home. Teach us to do everyday jobs with love for everybody in the whole family of Christ. Protect the worldwide church and draw us closer together. Amen.

Passover and
the Last Supper

Every year at Passover, Jewish families celebrate—with songs and story telling, special foods and prayers—the joyful event of Israel's deliverance from slavery in Egypt. The night before Jesus was crucified, he celebrated a traditional Passover meal with his disciples (who were all observant Jews, we need to remember), and it became the setting for the institution of the Eucharist. Many of our customs at Mass are rooted in the Passover ceremony (the priest's washing his hands and the elevation of the bread and wine, to name but two). The liturgy of Holy Week is filled with Passover references and symbols which will be impossible to miss once you've prepared for this echo story. If you want to make this activity even more memorable, be ready with a box of matzoh crackers to share during the discussion time afterward.

When Jesus was still walking the earth,
(walk in place)

he invited his disciples
(beckon: "Come here")

to eat the Passover meal with him.
(eating motions, happy face)

It was the night before he died.
(stretch out arms in crucifixion posture)

But they didn't know that,
(shake head)

or that it would be the Last Supper.
(shake head even more sadly)

So they were cheerful...
(perk up, pull corners of mouth up with fingers)

And they ran around getting ready.
(run excitedly in place)

Passover was a special time for the Jews.
(tap "wristwatch")

A time to remember
(tap forehead)

that Moses led their ancestors out of Egypt,
(turn to side, march in place, looking over shoulder)

and that the blood of a lamb on their doorposts
(reach up to smear blood on "doorposts")

made the angel of death
(flap arms as if wings)

pass over their houses
(make large arc with arm: "pass over")

on the night the firstborn of Egypt died.
(close eyes, droop head)

They escaped in the middle of the night.
(cup hands around eyes, trying to see)

And they left so quickly
(run in place, looking over shoulder)

that their bread didn't have time to rise.
(hold hands together, then indicate "rising" of bread)

They remembered that the waters of the Red Sea
(outline waves with hand)

made a wall to their *right*
(indicate big "wall" on the audience's right)

and a wall to their *left*,
(indicate "wall" on the left)

so they could cross over the Red Sea
(outline waves with hand)

on dry land.
(look down at feet as if puzzled, pick up foot experimentally)

Pharaoh's soldiers chased them,
(gallop in place)

but they drowned in the water.
(pinch nose with one hand, hold up other, make "blub, blub" sounds)

The Jews remember this every year
(tap forehead)

and celebrate with a special meal.
(eating motions, happy face)

God freed them from slavery
(cross wrists in front of self, then release as if breaking free)

and led them to the Promised Land.
(turn to side, march in place)

They "passed over" from slavery to freedom.
(make arc with arm: "pass over")

They "passed over" the Red Sea.
(make larger arc with arm: "pass over")

The angel of death "passed over" their houses.
(make huge arc with arm: "pass over")

Jesus and his friends were all Jews.
(put one hand on chest, then indicate "all" in group)

They loved the Passover feast.
(eating motions, happy face)

They loved thanking God for freedom.
(raise hands in praise)

It was like our Thanksgiving dinner,
(eating motions)

with special food and special prayers,
(fold hands in prayer)

lamb and wine and unleavened bread,
(make eating motions)

and beautiful prayers of blessing.
(fold hands in prayer)

So Jesus took the bread that night,
(hold up "bread" in both hands)

and the wine they were drinking,
(hold up "cup" with one hand, as in a toast)

and prayed the prayers of blessing.
(bow head, fold hands in prayer)

Then he said, "This is my Body,"
(point to "bread," then to self)

and, "This is my blood."
(point to "cup," then to self)

"Do this in remembrance of me."
(point to self with both hands)

The apostles were surprised.
(raise eyebrows, clap both hands to cheeks)

They didn't understand.
(shake head, puzzled)

But later they remembered it,
(tap forehead)

after Jesus died on the cross,
(stretch out arms in crucifixion posture)

and after he rose from the dead.
(slowly raise "crucified" arms over head)

They talked about it then.
(make "talking" signs with hands)

They understood the Last Supper more and more.
(tap forehead slowly, thoughtfully)

They understood Jesus was the new "Passover,"
(make large arc with arm: "pass over")

passing over from death to new life.
(make even larger arc with arm)

They remembered Jesus
(tap forehead)

in the breaking of the bread.
(hold up "bread" and break it in half)

And they told the story
(make "talking" signs with hands)

over and over again.
(roll forearms over each other)

They called it the "Eucharist,"
(elevate "host" as at Mass)

A new way of thanking God
(raise hands in praise)

for giving us Jesus and a new Passover.
(make arc with arm, "pass over")

We're just like the disciples...
(tap self on chest)

We don't understand at first,
(shake head, puzzled)

but we remember Jesus
(tap forehead)

in the breaking of the bread
(hold up "bread," break it)

every time we go to Mass.
(turn to side, walk in place determinedly)

Every time we receive communion,
(hold out hands, as if for communion)

we understand it more and more.
(tap forehead slowly)

We understand with our hearts...
(cross hands over heart)

And we understand with our hands...
(reach out with open, empty hands, as if for communion)

And also with our minds.
(tap forehead)

And we offer it all back to God
(point to heavens)

in thanks and praise.
(raise hands in praise)

We offer it all back to God
(point to heavens)

in thanks and praise.
(raise hands in praise, drop head with finality)

Questions for Discussion

Tell the children to sit down, and ask them questions like these:

- Does anyone you know celebrate Passover? Have you tasted any of the special foods, like matzoh crackers?

- Have you ever been to the special liturgy on Holy Thursday? What things were different?

- If Jesus invited you to a feast with him, would you come late and leave early like some people do for Mass? How would you get ready for a feast with Jesus?

- Do you know anyone who goes to daily Mass? Have you ever asked them why they love daily communion so much?

- Can you think of some things that were a mystery to you at first, but which you understood better as you grew older?

Closing Prayer

Lord Jesus, you longed to eat the Passover meal with your friends before you suffered and died, and you long to have us come to the table of your eucharist even to this day. Help us attend Mass with great reverence and never take it for granted. Enrich our love for this mystery, and keep us faithful until you bring us all to the Passover feast in heaven. Amen.

Simon Helps Jesus

Simon of Cyrene's viewpoint of the crucifixion is unique. In all likelihood he had never heard of Jesus when he was pressed into service to help carry the cross (Luke 23:26). Simon was just another Jewish pilgrim, a "man from the country" coming to Jerusalem to celebrate Passover. By a fluke of history he was caught up in events beyond his power to imagine. He became a believer as a result of his experience: Mark's gospel notes that he was the father of Alexander and Rufus, two Christians well known to the early church. In keeping with the reverence due any reenactment of the Passion, the teacher needs to exercise special care to make the tone of this echo story subdued and thoughtful. Pacing it slower than usual is one helpful hint.

Simon came in from the country one day,
(walk in place, look around, whistle)

looking forward to the Passover feast.
(rub tummy: "mmm")

He saw Roman soldiers on the road.
(shade eyes, look)

They were whipping a man who had fallen.
(make whipping motions)

Suddenly a soldier ran up to Simon
(run in place)

and grabbed him by the arm.
(fiercely grab one arm with your other hand)

He was marched over to the man in the road.
(march stiffly, arms at sides)

Simon didn't know it was Jesus.
(shake head, mystified)

But he saw his crown of thorns.
(draw crown around head)

And he saw the whip marks on his back.
(tip shoulder and point over back)

He saw a *big* cross on the ground.
(gesture to ground on "big," arms wide)

The soldiers made him lift it up,
(stoop, make lifting motions to pick it up)

and carry the cross behind Jesus.
(hoist cross on shoulder, walk heavily in place)

The cross got heavier and heavier,
(trudge more slowly, weighed down)

but Simon was very strong.
(flex muscles)

Some women were weeping and sobbing.
(bow head on arm, weep)

Jesus stopped and spoke to them.
(make "talking" motion with hand)

"Don't weep for me," he said.
(shake head, pointing to self)

"Weep for yourselves and your children."
(point to "them" and indicate "little ones")

Simon and Jesus carried the cross farther.
(hoist cross back on shoulder, walk in place)

Finally they put it down at Golgotha.
(tip "cross" and set down)

The soldiers made Jesus lie on the ground.
(point to ground, insistent)

They nailed his hands to the cross.
(make hammering motions on each outstretched palm)

And they nailed his feet.
(lean over, make more hammering motions on feet)

They pulled the cross up and Jesus hung there.
(stand with arms outstretched)

Simon didn't know what was happening.
(put hands on sides of face, shocked)

Who was this Jesus he had helped?
(scratch head, mystified)

The soldiers rolled dice for his tunic,
(pretend to shake dice, then roll)

a seamless garment, all in one piece.
(touch shirt, hold up one finger)

They gave Jesus vinegar to drink.
(make a sour face, turn away, stick out tongue)

They put a sign over his head,
(stretch imaginary sign over head)

"Jesus of Nazareth, King of the Jews."
(point to four "words" on imaginary sign over head)

Some people mocked and laughed at Jesus.
(slap thigh, pretending to laugh scornfully)

"Save yourself, if you're the Son of God!"
(point mockingly to heaven, and then indicate "come down")

Jesus spoke from the cross:
(stretch out arms as if crucified)

"Father, forgive them..."
(point to heaven, then offstage to "them")

"For they don't know what they're doing."
(shake head, sorrowfully)

Two thieves were crucified with Jesus.
(hold up two fingers)

One said, "Jesus, remember me..."
(point to self, humbly)

"When you come into your kingdom."
(point up to heaven, hopefully)

Jesus turned and said to him,
(stretch out "crucified arms," then turn head to side)

"Today you will be with me in paradise."
(point to "you" then to self then heavenward)

Simon still didn't know what was happening.
(put hands on sides of face, puzzled)

Who was this Jesus he had helped?
(stand and scratch head, mystified)

Then the sky got very dark.
(put arms over head, fearfully)

And Jesus breathed his last.
(stretch out arms, exhale, drop head to chest)

There was an earthquake.
(shake and reel and tip)

The Roman soldiers were afraid.
(cower, bite nails, chatter teeth)

"Truly this was the Son of God!" one said.
(nod head, point up to heaven, frightened)

Simon *still* did not understand.
(put hands on sides of face, puzzled)

Who *was* this Jesus he had helped?
(stand and scratch head)

They took the body down from the cross.
(reach up to "cross" then lower "body")

And carried it to a tomb.
(walk in place carrying "body")

They rolled a huge stone in front.
(push a heavy "stone")

And Roman soldiers stood guard.
(stand at attention, salute)

Simon walked sadly back to the city.
(turn to the side and walk slowly)

Three days later, everyone was talking.
(make "talking" motions, excited)

Jesus had risen from the dead!
(stretch out "crucified" arms, lift slowly upward in triumph)

He was the Messiah, the Son of God!
(point up to heaven)

So *that's* who Simon had helped!
(slap forehead lightly with hand)

Simon was so glad he had been there.
(cross arms over chest, bow head)

He thanked God for being able to help.
(keep head bowed, fold hands in prayer)

He thanked God for being able to help.
(keep head bowed, nod a few times, keep hands folded)

Questions for Discussion

With this subdued ending, let the children sit quietly for a minute, and perhaps show them a crucifix before beginning to ask these questions:

- Have you seen the fifth station of the cross in the church? What does it show?

- How do you feel when you're forced to help someone? How do you feel when you volunteer to help?

- Did you ever help someone who was sick or in pain?

- When you've been hurt, has anyone stopped and helped you? Were they kind?

- How can we remember to pray for people who've helped us?

Closing Prayer

Heavenly Father, you were so good to send Simon to help Jesus during his time of suffering. Help us be like Simon whenever we can help people carry their "cross." Remind us to be thankful to those who help us when we need a hand, and to pray for them. Open everybody's eyes, dear Father, so we can see and help all your people who are suffering in this world. Amen.

Mary Magdalene at the Tomb

Traditionally Mary Magdalene is the classic example of a penitent sinner because of Luke's story of the woman who bathed the feet of Jesus with her tears, dried them with her hair, and anointed them with expensive ointment (Luke 7:36–50). In the Scriptures the woman in this incident is not actually named, though artists continue to picture Mary Magdalene with long hair and an alabaster jar. Mary Magdalene *is* mentioned by name, however, as a disciple of Jesus in his ministry, and for her heroic presence at the crucifixion, burial, and resurrection. Her feast day is July 22. Her witness to the Resurrection as given in this echo pantomime is taken almost entirely from John 20, which older students might want to read.

Easter Sunday, very early in the morning,
(rub eyes as if waking up)

Mary Magdalene woke up
(stretch, rub eyes some more)

and gathered together some ointments
(gather things into "basket" over arm)

to anoint the body of Jesus.
(rub "oil" on arms, then torso)

She had loved Jesus with her whole heart.
(cross hands over heart)

She saw him die on the cross.
(stretch out arms like a cross)

And she saw them put him in the tomb
(shade eyes to watch)

and roll a huge stone in front.
(make pushing motions on "stone")

Afterward she sat there,
(pantomime sitting, dazed)

just watching and weeping.
(bow head on arms, weep)

She had loved Jesus with her whole heart.
(cross hands over heart)

And was sad when he died.
(pull down corners of mouth)

But now she could anoint Jesus' body,
(rub "oil" on arms, then torso)

so she hurried to the tomb.
(run in place)

But when she got there,
(stop abruptly after running, shocked)

she couldn't believe her eyes!
(look aghast, hands on cheeks)

The stone had been rolled away.
(make pushing motions on "stone")

The tomb was empty!
(turn hands up, amazed)

Mary ran back to tell Peter and John.
(run in place, facing right)

They came quickly to see for themselves.
(run in place, facing left)

They poked their heads inside the tomb.
(bend and stick head "in," look around)

The burial cloth was all rolled up,
(make rolling motions with hands)

but Jesus wasn't there.
(shake head, amazed)

Peter and John couldn't figure it out,
(stand there dumbfounded, scratching head)

so they turned and went home.
(turn 180 degrees around and walk in place)

But Mary Magdalene stayed behind, weeping.
(bow head on arm, weep)

She had loved Jesus with her whole heart.
(cross hands over heart)

And she didn't know where his body was.
(shake head)

Then she saw two angels sitting there.
(flap arms like wings)

"Why are you weeping?" they said.
(turn hands up, questioning)

"They've taken my Lord," she told them.
(point offstage, puzzled)

"And I don't know where they put him."
(shake head, shrug shoulders sadly)

Then she turned around and saw a man.
(turn to face other direction, shade eyes with hand)

It was Jesus, but she didn't know it.
(shake head and tap forehead, wonderingly)

"Why are you weeping," the man said.
(shrug, turn hands up, questioning)

Mary thought he was the gardener.
(make motions as if pruning, or digging)

"Sir, if *you* carried him away..."
(point to "you")

"Tell me and *I* will take him."
(point to self)

Jesus said one word: "Mary."
(hold up one finger, speak lovingly)

Immediately Mary knew it was Jesus.
(clap hands to cheeks in astonishment)

She knew with her whole heart he was alive!
(cross hands over heart)

She fell at his feet.
(kneel and embrace Jesus' "feet")

"Don't cling to me," said Jesus.
(shake head and ward her off)

"I haven't ascended to the Father yet."
(point up to heaven)

"Go back to my disciples"
(point offstage)

"and tell them what I've told you."
(make "talking" motion with hand)

Mary ran back to the disciples
(run in place, excitedly)

and did what Jesus asked.
(make "talking" motions with hand)

"I have seen the Lord!" she said.
(tap upper cheekbones, pointing to own eyes)

"I have seen the Lord!"
(point to eyes, again and again, excited)

The disciples didn't believe her at first.
(shake head, make "dismissing" motions)

They didn't understand about Jesus rising.
(tap forehead and shake head)

But Mary believed with her whole heart.
(cross hands over heart)

She was the first to see him risen.
(hold up one finger)

Then Jesus showed himself to others.
(tap chest with both hands, "showing self," turning)

He walked to Emmaus with two of his apostles.
(walk in place)

They recognized him when he broke bread.
(hold up "bread" and break it)

Then he let Thomas touch his wounds.
(touch right side of torso, then palms of hands)

And once he ate fish with them on the beach.
(eating motions, smack lips: "mmm")

But Mary had believed with her whole heart.
(cross hands over heart)

And she was the first to see him risen.
(hold up one finger)

Jesus walked around for forty days,
(walk in place, gesture as if talking)

showing himself to many people.
(tap chest with both hands, "showing self," turning)

Then he ascended into heaven.
(slowly raise eyes up, pointing upwards)

But Mary Magdalene was the first to see him risen.
(hold up one finger)

She had loved him with her whole heart.
(cross hands over heart)

Questions for Discussion

Have the students sit down and answer some of the following questions after you have finished the echo story:

- Do you like to wake up earlier than everybody else? What things do you see very early in the morning?

- Have you ever rubbed good-smelling lotions and oils on your skin?

- Why do you think Mary Magdalene had a hard time recognizing that the "gardener" was Jesus?

- What do you do when people don't believe you at first, like the disciples who didn't believe Mary Magdalene?

- How can you show Jesus that you love him with your whole heart?

Closing Prayer

Risen Lord Jesus, thank you for showing yourself to Mary Magdalene who loved you so much she wanted to be the first at your tomb Easter morning. Give us her eagerness to follow you everywhere and her courage to tell others about you. Don't let us get discouraged by the things that make us sad and the people who won't believe. Help us take the initiative and be first in line to serve you. Amen.

What's a Paraclete?

The Holy Spirit is too often the "forgotten person of the Trinity," and the feast of Pentecost is too often lost in the hectic demands of the end of the school year. This echo story hopes to amend both situations. After using it your class won't forget that the word paraclete means "right-by-your-side" almost literally, in Greek, and that the word Pentecost means "fifty." Some versions of the Bible translate paraclete as "advocate," which is also correct, but we think the image of having the Holy Spirit "right-by-your-side" is a comforting one for all ages. Older students might want to read for themselves the details of the first Pentecost (Acts 2), and the words of Jesus about who the Holy Spirit is (especially John 14, 15, 16).

It was *fifty* days after Easter.
(slowly flash ten fingers, five times)

Jesus had already ascended into heaven.
(move face, arms slowly upward, lift body to tiptoe)

All his friends were scared.
(cower, bite fingernails, chatter teeth)

Jesus had said, *"Wait* for the Paraclete."
(move palms downward as in "Settle down!")

"But what's a Paraclete?" they wondered.
(shrug, look puzzled, palms upward)

They wanted Jesus back again, right by their side.
(pat side)

They were together in an upstairs room
(make step-climbing motions)

and were frightened
(cower, bite nails)

and trying to pray...
(fold hands, bow head)

trying to remember what Jesus had told them.
(tap forehead, pondering)

"The Holy Spirit is like the *wind*," he had said.
(blow, "Whoosh!")

"You can hear the sound,"
(cup hand to ear)

"but you don't know where it's coming from..."
(peer off to left)

"Or where it's going."
(swing head and peer off to right)

"*Wait* for the Paraclete."
(move palms downward as in "Settle down!")

"But what's a Paraclete?" they said.
(shrug, look puzzled, palms upward)

They wanted Jesus back again, right by their side.
(pat side)

"The Holy Spirit will give you *understanding*," Jesus said.
(tap forehead)

"The Holy Spirit will give you *power* from above."
(raise clenched "power" fist)

"The Holy Spirit will teach you what to say."
(make "talking" gesture)

"So *wait* for the Paraclete."
(move palms downward as in "Settle down!")

"But *what is* a Paraclete?" they wondered.
(shrug, look puzzled, get impatient)

They wanted Jesus back, right by their side!
(pat side more insistently)

"The Holy Spirit is like *breath*," Jesus had said.
(breathe in, breathe out)

"The breath that gives you *life*."
(stretch, do exercises, wiggle)

"The breath that calls out *Abba, Father*."
(reach up to heaven in gesture of praise)

"The breath that helps you *forgive*."
(shake hands in sign of peace)

"So *wait* for the Paraclete."
(move palms downward as in "Settle down!")

"But WHAT IS A PARACLETE?" they wondered.
(shrug, fold arms across chest, be demanding)

They wanted Jesus back, right by their side.
(pat side, demandingly)

"The Holy Spirit will give you *courage*," Jesus said.
(step forward, boldly flex muscles)

"The Holy Spirit will give you *joy*."
(use fingers to make mouth into happy face)

"The Holy Spirit will teach you the deep things of God."
(with hand, make spiral motions downwards)

"The Holy Spirit will give you the *peace* that passes understanding."
(hands across heart)

"So *wait* for the Paraclete."
(move palms downward as in "Settle down!")

"We can't wait ANY LONGER!" they said.
(insistent, jump up and down as if in a tantrum)

They still didn't know what a Paraclete was.
(shake head vigorously, puzzled)

But, boy, did they want one!
(nod vigorously)

So they prayed harder and harder.
(fold hands, close eyes fervently)

Suddenly the house shook like an earthquake.
(shake all over, reel, lurch)

A loud *wind* blew.
(make "Woooooo" sound, blowing)

And *tongues of fire* came on top of their heads.
(point to top of heads of everybody in room)

They all started talking at the same time.
(make "talking" gesture)

They were all talking *different* languages.
(turn "talking" gestures toward self, look puzzled)

They ran outside to tell everyone.
(run in place, excitedly)

People from all over the world were there.
(make expansive gesture, a circle)

Everyone heard their *own* language.
(cup ear, nod with understanding)

They were amazed.
(clap both hands to cheeks)

"They're all *drunk*," someone said.
(make drinking gestures, act tipsy)

"But it's only nine o'clock in the morning!" said Peter.
(tap wristwatch indignantly)

"The Holy Spirit came down on us."
(reach hands over head, then settle on top in shape of flame)

"It's the Spirit of Jesus, right by our side!"
(pat side excitedly)

"We're not afraid anymore!"
(shake head decisively)

"We want the whole world to know."
(make expansive gesture, completing a circle)

"We want everybody to be baptized."
(mime pouring water over heads)

"And have their sins forgiven."
(shake hands in peace sign)

"And receive the Holy Spirit."
(blow "whoooosh" gently)

"The Holy Spirit of Jesus, right by our side!"
(pat side proudly)

"Now we *know* who the Paraclete is!"
(hold up forefinger in "I've got it!" sign)

"It's the Spirit of Jesus, right by our side!"
(pat all up and down side enthusiastically)

That day they baptized three thousand people.
(mime pouring water over lots and lots of people)

And the Church was born.
(rock baby in arms, look at it proudly)

Pentecost is the Church's birthday...
(stoop and pretend to blow candles)

Fifty days after Easter.
(slowly flash ten fingers, five times)

Pentecost means "fifty."
(flash ten fingers faster and faster)

Praise God for the Paraclete...
(raise hands in praise)

The Spirit of Jesus right by our side.
(pat side excitedly and proudly)

PRAISE GOD FOR THE PARACLETE...
(shout, raise hands higher in praise)

THE SPIRIT OF JESUS RIGHT BY OUR SIDE.
(shout, pat side more forcefully)

Praise God for the Paraclete.
(whisper, raise hands more humbly)

The Spirit of Jesus, right by our side.
(whisper, patting side very gently, repeat)

Questions for Discussion

Settle the children down and let them ask questions about the Holy Spirit and Pentecost.

- Isn't everybody afraid sometimes? Is it less scary when you know Jesus is right by your side?

- Do you remember a time when you were brave and had courage? How did you act?

- How many things can you think of that you know about without being able to see them? (air, sound, fragrance, germs, emotions, faraway places...)

- How can we celebrate the birthday of the church?

- Try to make up your own prayer asking for the help of the Holy Spirit.

Closing Prayer

Come, Holy Spirit, fill us with your surprising gifts and teach us how to use them to build up the church. Make us all grow in holiness and unity as you sanctify our uniqueness. Pour out a spirit of wisdom on our generation so that all human beings will be drawn into the embrace of our loving Father. We pray all this in Jesus' name. Amen.

Of Related Interest...

20 Prayer Lessons for Children

PHYLLIS VOS WEZEMAN
AND JUDE DENNIS FOURNIER

Here is a fun and faith-filled guide to teaching prayer. Each simple and direct lesson centers around an activity designed to bring out a particular prayer theme. Activities include drama, dance, games, music, storytelling and art.

ISBN: 0-89622-689-1, 64 pp, $9.95

Jesus For Children

WILLIAM GRIFFIN

Each Bible story is told in children's language, retaining the biblical names and the original flavor of the gospel. The large type and full-page illustrations make for easy out-loud reading.

ISBN: 0-89622-610-7, 144 pp, $9.95

Ways to Pray with Children

Prayers, Activities, and Services
BARBARA ANN BRETHERTON

This resource for teachers, catechists, and parents teaches how to make prayer practical, enjoyable, easily accessible, and relevant in the lives of children. Offers suggestions on incorporating prayer into children's lives and describes many different forms of prayer.

ISBN: 0-89622-670-0, 80 pp, $9.95

Weekday Liturgies For Children

Creative Ways to Celebrate Year-Round
MARY KATHLEEN GLAVICH, SND

The author provides guidelines and suggestions for making liturgies more interesting and appealing to children while involving them in the celebration. Her book includes themes, suggestions for intercessions, homily guidelines, and many ways to vary the singing, prayers, and other parts of the Mass.

ISBN: 0-89622-694-8, 240 pp, $29.95

Prayer Themes and Guided Meditations for Children

BARBARA ANN BRETHERTON

The author offers guidelines for 16 imaginative and prayerful meditation experiences. Each has four basic steps: a relaxation activity, a guide to focusing on an object or objects related to the theme, a reflection upon the theme or object of prayer, and an invitation to prayer. The meditations vary in length and style. They provide the teacher or parent with a variety of approaches for different levels of ability and maturity. The language, concepts, and ideas are adaptable and may be simplified or extended as needed. The themes of these meditations include: "God Things," "Jesus' Mom Is My Mom," "Earth Care," and "I Believe in Angels."

ISBN 0-89622-896-7, 96 pp, $9.95

Available at religious bookstores or from:

XXIII TWENTY-THIRD PUBLICATIONS
P.O. BOX 180 • MYSTIC, CT 06355

1-800-321-0411 • E-Mail:ttpubs@aol.com